COLLEGE FAST TRACK

Other Books

Also by Derrick Hibbard

Law School Fast Track: Essential Habits for Law School Success

For the Law Student

The Art of the Law School Transfer: A Guide to Transferring Law Schools

The Insider's Guide to Getting a Big Firm Job: What Every Law Student Should Know About Interviewing

Later-in-Life Lawyers: Tips for the Non-Traditional Law Student

Law School: Getting In, Getting Good, Getting the Gold

Law School Undercover: A Veteran Law Professor Tells the Truth About Admissions, Classes, Cases, Exams, Law Review, and More

Planet Law School II: What You Need to Know (Before You Go)—but Didn't Know to Ask…and No One Else Will Tell You

The Slacker's Guide to Law School: Success Without Stress

For the New Lawyer

Jagged Rocks of Wisdom: Professional Advice for the New Attorney

Jagged Rocks of Wisdom—The Memo: Mastering the Legal Memorandum

Jagged Rocks of Wisdom—Negotiation: Mastering the Art of the Deal

Jagged Rocks of Wisdom—Contracts: Mastering the Art of Contract Drafting (forthcoming)

The Young Lawyer's Jungle Book: A Survival Guide

Non-Law Adventures

Grains of Golden Sand: Adventures in War-Torn Africa

Training Wheels for Student Leaders: A Junior Counseling Program in Action

COLLEGE FAST TRACK

ESSENTIAL HABITS FOR LESS STRESS AND MORE SUCCESS IN COLLEGE

DERRICK HIBBARD

THE FINE PRINT PRESS

HONOLULU

Copyright © 2011 by Derrick Hibbard

Published by
The Fine Print Press, Ltd.
Honolulu, Hawaii
Website: www.fineprintpress.com
Email: info@fineprintpress.com

Library of Congress Cataloging-in-Publication Data

Hibbard, Derrick, 1983-
    College fast track : essential habits for law school success /
    Derrick Hibbard.
        p. cm.
    ISBN 978-1-888960-23-5 (softcover : alk. paper)
    1. College student orientation—Juvenile literature. I. Title.
LB2343.3.H53 2011
378.1'98--dc22

                            2011006104

Cover design and typesetting by Designwoerks, Wichita, Kansas.
Editing by Chad Pickering and Thane Messinger.

The text face is Esprit Book, designed by Jovica Veljović and issued by ITC in 1985; supplemented with chapter headings in Castellar, designed by John Peters and issued by Monotype in 1957, section headings in Poppl-Laudatio, designed in 1982 by Friedrich Poppl for the H. Berthold AG Typefoundry of Berlin, and accent uses of American Typewriter, Helvetica Neue, and Law & Order.

PRINTED IN THE UNITED STATES OF AMERICA
20 19 18 17 16 15 14 13 12 11   9 8 7 6 5 4 3 2 1

Contents

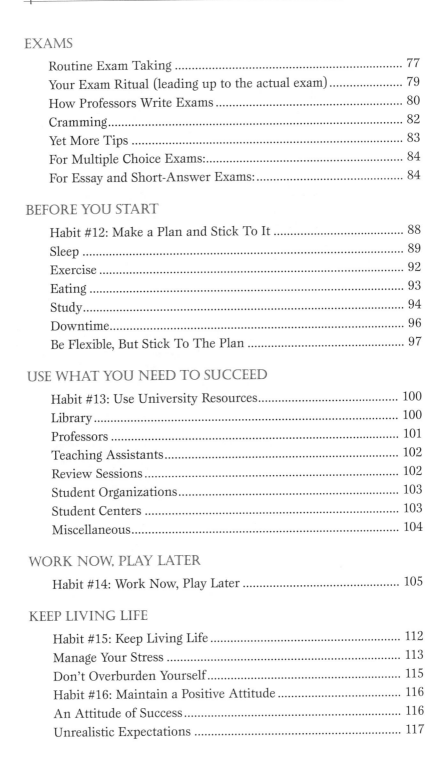

EXAMS

BEFORE YOU START

USE WHAT YOU NEED TO SUCCEED

WORK NOW, PLAY LATER

KEEP LIVING LIFE

For Adelaide Bleu, born just minutes ago.

Acknowledgments

A special thanks to my family. Without the support of Amanda, Zoe, Liam, and Adelaide, this book, as well as my experience in college and in law school, would not have been possible.

To Scott Nelson and Debbie Every, fantastic teachers and mentors who believed in me when it was all a dream.

To my dad and mom, for constantly encouraging me; for instilling in me many of the habits that you find in this book; and for their many encouragements—not least that of education.

To Darin Gates and Codell Carter, who made difficult concepts accessible—and the most tedious subjects, interesting.

To Cyndee Frazier, Matthew Holland, Charles Swift, and Cal Aaronson, all of whom rounded out my college experience and made it memorable.

To Ben Esco, whose advice on juggling multiple tasks is found here in this book.

Finally, to Thane Messinger for his extraordinary advice and support in this whole process.

FOREWORD

College is many things.

For a percentage of students, college is the culmination of an intellectual dream: the chance to think, think, *think!* Not just that, but college is a mostly protected world—perhaps the first such a person has ever known—in which it is okay to be really, really smart.

For another, larger group, college is a chance to escape—the last and possibly best time in one's life with a maximum of freedom and a minimum of rules and responsibilities. For a member of this group, college is one big party.

For many, college is something of an expected rite of passage—just something to go through, something expected on the way to a job, career, mortgage, and so on.

For some, college is a source of deep anxiety, either because it is an experience foreign to one's family background, or because of financial pressures, or because of genuine physiological distress, or for any of a dozen other reasons.

The truth about college is some version of *All of the Above.* In ages past, college was the realm of the wealthy and connected, with a smattering of the bright and exceptionally ambitious. Few could afford tuition (which was relatively modest by comparison to today's rates). Fewer still could afford to defer day-to-day household expenses for even a year, much less four. Work was simply an expectation, often from an age far younger than would seem possible today. This was especially true in the early age of industrialization, where hands and muscle (not enlightened citizen-employees) were needed on farms and in factories. For many, higher education was simply not in the picture. And so, we should be more appreciative (at least) of the far wider opportunities now open to us.

Whatever your particular circumstance or expectation, it is important to know going in what college will be, and how to best fit in and take advantage of its many lessons and adventures.

* * *

College is more than mere academics. This should come as no surprise, as many (if not most) college students are focused in those numerous extracurricular activities.

Purists will of course object. College is about academics! Well, yes. But if it were simply "academic," why go at all? After all, one could read the best ten books in each field, take a test, and we would have real proof that the person would know as much (if not more) than an actual college graduate.

You might have seen the *Saturday Night Live* skit in which Father Guido Sarducci, cigarette in hand, offers the Five Minute University:

> You know, in college you have to take a foreign language. Well, at the Five Minute University you can have your choice—any language you want, you can take it. Say if you want to take Spanish, what I teach you is *"¿Como está usted?"* That means, "How are you?" The answer is *"muy bien,"* which means "very well." And believe me, if you took two years of college Spanish, five years after you are out of school *"¿Como está usted?"* and *"muy bien"* about all you're gonna' remember.

The open secret is that, as an intellectual enterprise, college is not exactly the most efficient model. And so, for anyone about to enter college, the world beyond the academic is also worth thinking about...and planning for. This is among Hibbard's contributions, as his focus on building good habits will afford you the time to truly enjoy all those fun, extra-academic activities—while succeeding on the academic side as well (and remembering more than just *"¿Como está usted?"* and *"¡Muy bien!"*).

There is for everyone the chirpy adage that "College is what you make of it."

Well, yes. College *is* what you make of it. Many graduates look back on their years in college with a mixture of wistfulness and regret. If only they'd taken a different major...if only they'd enjoyed themselves more...if only...if only....

Other graduates look back on their college years with a smile. They had a great time, and they built the credentials that served them well in the years to come.

Your task is to be in the latter group. Hibbard's book is a step in that direction. He offers some surprising gems—truths that we not only don't often think about, but truths we might not even realize unless someone points them out.

One of them is his advice to be only *mostly right.*

Wow.

One could go a lifetime and never realize this fundamental truth. In fact, one could spend years in a corporate world and bounce from one saccharine seminar to the next, all extolling them to "Give 110%!" and "Be the best!!" and so on. Those aren't wrong, exactly, but the deeper truth is that it's so much more important to be sure that you're focused in the right direction, first. This threshold question is missing in most other advice, because the concern is so overwhelmingly just to be "perfect."

For most, this is a false hope, and a false goal. Here's why: First, it is unlikely we'll ever know our "perfect" goal up front. Second, even if we did, it's likely it would change by the time we got there. Third, the reality for many is heard in another adage, this from Voltaire: *Don't let the perfect be the enemy of the good.* In other words, don't get caught up in trying to be perfect, so that you trip yourself up. Yes, you must do well, and yes, that takes some doing. But perfection, even if possible, requires so much additional effort that it's often simply not worth it. Sure, if at some point you're designing spacecraft then your definition of "perfect" is going to be rather strict, and you darned well better be striving for perfection; but for college—happily—the bar is set lower. Fourth, getting tripped up is exactly what happens to many. Precisely because being "perfect" is hard (well, impossible), we fail in frustration, when all we really needed was to be *almost* perfect. Fifth, *almost perfect* is not only more attainable, it is, paradoxically, likely to be better. It is almost certainly likely to be more fun. Sixth, in most instances "perfect" misses the point. Life and college are not "the answer." It's the ride, not always the destination. Finally, perfection *is* a goal, but...not yet. Even if you're a perfectionist, keep in mind the more-reasonable objectives of college. This might be all the more true *especially* if you're a perfectionist.

Stop trying to be perfect. Focus instead on continual improvement, in every aspect of your life. Don't insist on being "right"; expect of yourself instead to be *mostly* right. You'll find your quality improving more than when you set false goals, and you'll find yourself enjoying that quality all the more.

* * *

And to more of the actual advice:

Some of Hibbard's advice seems clichéd, even trite, such as "Set Goals and Follow Up."

Well, duh. Yet that doesn't make it any less true, and we find, time and again, that we get into trouble when we start forgetting the basics. Hibbard offers us these basics, in useful, usable ways.

Some of Hibbard's advice is of the general nagging variety, such as "Write Every Day."

Along with brushing our teeth, this is one of those constants that can be just plain annoying...until later when we realize we're in trouble. With teeth, this is when they start to fall out. With English, in truth sometimes we never know, because no one likes to tell another person they really can't communicate—but it makes a *big* difference in more ways than you'll know. A job promotion that doesn't happen is just the most obvious (and painful) of lessons, even if we never know why.

Yes, write every day. And not just any kind of "writing." I have worked with students for years. I see students who struggle with proper English—and not just "at risk" students. Even top students face challenges. Our world is changing, and even students who are in their element online find themselves suddenly struggling with formal writing assignments. The key is that your bosses will, most likely, be in the old element. Your professors (who will have some power over your success) still care about English, in large part because *they* write every day. Their standards are not loose. So, writing every day—proper, formal English—will help you in both worlds.

Some of Hibbard's advice seems common sense—but isn't really. For example, when he tells you to "be active in class," this doesn't mean what it usually means to someone who's just survived twelve years of schooling. It's important to be the *right kind* of active. Hibbard shows you how.

Some of Hibbard's advice is radical, such as on how to take notes—or, more correctly, how *not* to take notes. Read these sections especially carefully, as they can help you in class, on exams, *and* in saving lots and lots of time.

Some of Hibbard's advice is a different kind of radical, such as his advice on outlining. Few college students do outlines, in part because they're not part of the collegiate culture, in part because they're seen as too much work (they're actually less work), and in part because most students have gotten away without them. But just because something has always worked before does not mean that that's the way it should be done. Outlining can be an extraordinarily effective tool.

A quick story to show this point: Once upon a time, I saw notes my sister had made. She was taking zoology. I wasn't expecting much, as zoology was of only mild interest. I was blown away. Instead of boring notes about aardvarks and amoebae, zebras and zygotes, she had done detailed illustrations, in color! (She's quite an artist. In fact, some of her work is in a book she did about her adventures in the real world of zoology: *Grains of Golden Sand: Adventures in War-Torn Africa.*) I was transfixed. She had done far more than merely "learn" the course materials: she had brought them to life. It was a 1980s version of *Harry Potter,* where the newsprint articles are live-action holograms.

Clearly not everyone will produce outlines with color illustrations—but if you can, or something similar, you too will bring your course material to life. Among many other benefits, your grades will soar.

Some of Hibbard's advice seems ho-hum, such as his instruction to "plan one day per week to review for each final." Ho-hum it may be, but effective too.

And some of Hibbard's advice is profound, such as his Habit #14 ("Work Now, Play Later"). Something that was told to me by a professor many years ago has resonated for years: Work hard for four years, and your life is almost assured. Goof off for those four years, and you're likely to struggle for forty.

The problem is…we tend to see the world in either/or terms:

either we have fun *or* we work our tail off. No. First, we need to be clear on what "fun" means. While it certainly means different things to different people, *fun* is not the same as "goof off." This is an important distinction to keep in mind. You *should* work hard in college. If you're doing it right, it *is* work. You should also have fun in college. Lots of it.

"Work" in college is the best kind of work: you get to *think!* But if, overall, you're having "fun" to the extent that you're not actually *thinking* when you're supposedly working (studying)—which can be defined as being mentally tired at the end of each day from absorbing and thinking about whatever it is you're studying—you're not "having fun." You're simply goofing off.

Hibbard shows you how you can have the best of both: learning that is both effective and efficient, and, because of that, plenty of time left over for guilt-free fun.

The truth is…most of us did not do as good a job in college as we could have. We certainly didn't manage our time and mental energies as well as we could have. As a result, even if we did well we tended to work too hard to achieve those results.

It's easy to read these words and assume these are just nagging from some old fart who's forgotten what it's like. Perhaps. Yet the danger is not that if you follow what Hibbard suggests you'll become some sort of mindless automaton. The danger is that if you *don't* follow his advice, you'll never realize how much easier and better it could have been.

There are those who have worked very, very hard in college. Some even have extraordinary additional concerns, such as a family with children…yet these are the students who tend to excel. You're reading a book written by just such a person.

Another story if I might, from the book *Law School: Getting In, Getting Good, Getting the Gold.* While that book was about law school, the story itself is about a college student.

Picture a college classroom in a galaxy far, far away:

> You've heard of the expression "If you want something done, give it to a busy person?" Well, having taught many thousands of students, I can spot a certain type of stellar student within the first few meetings (if not the first few minutes). This is the person for whom an "A" is actually a

low standard—but not because of the grade. Rather, instead of focusing on the grade they're focused in the material. When others whine and moan about how much they have to do and how overloaded they are, these few students seem to magically produce what everyone else merely promises.

Often, I learn that these star students actually have more demanding lives than nearly all of the other students in the class. Just such as student apologized for being ten minutes late. She was an immigrant who was raising four children—the youngest in diapers—and working probably 80 hours per week at her family's store.

These are the students who excel. How can this be? Because they're efficient (they have to be) and because they spend less time moping and more time doing. This isn't an implicit insult if this isn't you, but it *is* a gentle nudge toward a better perspective. Following Hibbard's advice will be the practical support underneath that broader perspective.

Make college an *experience*. Make it something you look back on with pride:

"I *did* this! I learned what interested me; took an extra minor in something else I really liked; got great grades; made life-long friends; found a neat hobby; got into grad school; and had a *great* time. What a fantastic set of years!"

And, lest we forget another of the To Do items for college:

Have a great love affair!

Romance is part of college. Paradoxically, the better you do, the better will be your romance. As much as you'll be distracted while you're in love, having to worry about academic probation is not terribly romantic. Having already done well when you fall in love will give you academic breathing room.

You do not, as well, want to write in your graduate school application something to the effect that "I fell in love and my grades tanked." That is not only not an excuse, for admissions officers it's a marker of someone who is *not* ready for graduate school—or at least not their graduate school—wherein managing multiple responsibilities is more or less a daily requirement.

With this book, your college years are more likely to be ones *you* look back on fondly and with a sense of accomplishment. More importantly, these are years you're more likely to actually enjoy.

In your journey, may you look back with a smile.

Thane J. Messinger

Law School: Getting In, Getting Good, Getting the Gold

The Young Lawyer's Jungle Book: A Survival Guide

Spring 2011

WHY THIS BOOK

You are holding this book in your hands, flipping through the pages—or reading the comments and reviews online—and are probably wondering what separates this book from the rest. You could search the terms "college guide" or "tips for college" and hundreds of books and websites appear, many claiming to be the number one source of advice on how to do well in college. Among so many choices, you will inevitably ask, "Why *this* book?"

College is a new experience, socially even more than academically. It can be difficult. All who go to college (especially if they are far from home for the first time) will undergo serious personal adjustments during their first days, weeks, and months where they realize that college is *different*. It is different from high school, and to succeed you really do have to study. But that's not really the difference. The difference is that "study" in college isn't like the study you've done before. Study in college requires a new form of discipline, because professors will not provide the daily and weekly feedback that was routine before.

For most, college is the first time in their lives when their performance is based entirely on themselves. And once they've been to college, they'll look back and wish they would have studied differently, more effectively, or just *learned how to study*. This sounds odd, I know, but "study" is not automatic, and it's not the same as you're used to. Not everyone gets it right—especially at first. Among other things, most of us waste a lot of time when we *think* we're studying effectively, but when exams come along we realize just how poorly we "studied." This worked in high school, where there was a fairly broad spectrum of academic talent in each classroom; in college, though, only the better students are even *in* the classroom. They are your new competition.

Sometimes, the disconnect between the way college is and the way new students think it is (or think it should be) is great enough that they don't make it. Most students certainly don't do as well as they could, and many don't enjoy college nearly as much as they might with better habits. You read that correctly—this is not a guide to simply grind away at classes, homework, and late-night projects while everyone else seems to be having a good time.

This book is about getting good—even great—grades while still taking time to enjoy life as a college student. There are many good books out there, along with much good advice. This book will also help, but in a different way.

ABOUT COLLEGE

Your college years ought to be among the best times in your life, and also ought to be a solid stepping stone to whatever else you want to do in your future. In many cases, that "whatever else" is going to depend upon how well you did in college. But, of course, once you're in your senior year it's difficult (if not impossible) to undo years of poor grades. It's even harder to undo years of poor habits.

In applying for a graduate program, for example, your entire record is open to inspection, and graduate admissions committees *will* look seriously not only at your major, but also at your cours-es, grades, and even combinations of workloads, grades, and demands of each course. Their perspective is this: you *say* you will make a good [physician, attorney, economist, whatever]. But can you *show* that you know what it takes? Can you prove through your existing academic work that you *actually* handled difficult courses, that you did well, and that you can also handle the sort of workload in graduate school?

Say you don't want to go to graduate school. Chances are, if you would like to work at a top employer out of college, the interview-ers will be asking themselves the same questions. They might not be looking from the same academic standpoint, but they will want to know that you'll do a good job, handle a heavy workload, and do so consistently—without getting into trouble. If your transcript shows highly uneven results, or too many "gut courses," or any-thing else indicating poor habits, you're going to be at a serious dis-advantage as compared to someone who did have consistently good grades, in hard as well as easy courses.

Also, what if you decide later that you'd like to get a graduate or professional degree? In many companies, a bachelor's degree is just an entry; you'll need more to get promoted. Let's say you decide to get an MBA. Most top MBA programs require not only a few years of work experience—they also look at, yes, all of the factors mentioned above. Even if you think you won't care about grades, or if you think a B-average will be "good enough," chances are this will keep popping up as an issue, especially as you get started in your career. Among many other factors, how well you do will make a big difference in what initial opportunities are open to you—and which ones are not.

The first aim of this book is to uncover how you can have it all, or at least how you can balance good study habits with a fair amount of fun. This is not cold-hearted advice from some party pooper. It's from someone who has been through this whole process, and who then went through the same process at an even more intense level in law school.

SAYS WHO?

I remember preparing to begin college—not too long ago—which is one reason this advice is so applicable. Unlike some other guides, this book is not written by someone long past the actual experience, or by a professor or dean or administrator who's looking at the world very differently than does a student.

I read several of those other guides, and while they were helpful, they often provided too *much* information. They did explain the college experience, but I didn't want to be told what college was like; I'd seen many movies about the college experience and had a general idea of what it entailed. I wanted and needed quick answers about simple things—questions such as how to get the most out my studies, or how many notes is too many notes, or how to prepare, day in and day out, for quizzes and exams. I ended up wasting time reading about things I didn't really need to know—or things that were self-explanatory.

Eventually I had to cut through the mass of details to find what I really needed. Often, this was through trial and error—an inefficient way to learn. So while I did well, my efforts were inefficient;

I thus ended up working less effectively (and harder) than I had to. The point of this brief guide is to cut through that mass of details *for you*. Obviously there are many things to think about in college—after all, this is the launch pad for the rest of your life. This book will give you the basic principles that will help you *right now*. And if you implement the advice in this book *right now*, then you will benefit down the road when you're applying to graduate school or for your first professional job. This book provides you with the *essential* habits to succeed in college.

THE BOOK

Even the table of contents in this book is set up to help you reach your highest level of effective productivity. Thumb through the table. If there are already parts at which you are proficient, then by all means, skip that section! Do not waste your time reading about good habits you have already developed. You might, however, first confirm that your habits really are *good* habits; many of us have a falsely positive view of just how effective and efficient our habits are.

The book is also designed to be easily accessible when you want to correct or improve specific habits. Four years is a long time. Good habits will last—if you consciously and consistently stick with them—but bad habits are likely to creep in (or creep back) all the same. As the saying goes, this isn't rocket science. There are reasons we tend to get sloppy, changing our lives from mostly good habits to mostly bad ones. There are many forces pulling us away from good habits, and toward bad ones. Use this book as your tool for becoming more efficient *and* more effective as a student.

THE LIST

The list of essential habits in this book is short, and purposely so. There are books out there that advertise "101 habits for students" or even "1001 things to know about college." While many of those habits are good, and most assuredly there are good habits mixed in the jumble, it is important not to be inundated with trying to do too much—your success will get lost in that jumble.

No, this book has a short list of habits—only the *essential* habits. These are, however, the habits that will lead to your success and allow you the freedom and time to actually enjoy yourself, without panicking over whether or not you've "studied enough," can take the time off, or are even on the right track.

WHY HABITS?

Habits help us. Or they can hurt us.

Good habits help in everyday life, in the many day-to-day things we have to do. Being a student is really no different. When you develop good habits that help you accomplish your goals and tasks quickly and well, you will be more successful. It's important, however, to get beyond the thinking that good habits are "hard" and bad habits are "easy"; sometimes that's true, but often it is not. Many times, a good habit is simply doing things logically, proactively, and with care. Well, okay…not "simply." It's easy to *say* we'll build good habits; the challenge is to actually *do* that.

A habit is something you do without needing to think. In college you will need to think—a lot—but you will also need to focus your energies on immediate tasks and goals, as well as on your future. Many times we're not exactly sure what *specific* tasks we should focus on, or even what our goals (or future) should be, so it's not surprising that our habits are not always good ones. Developing these good habits will help you as a student, allowing you to focus better on actual learning. Grades are a reflection of that. Success will come.

Although the advice in this book will ultimately make your work as a student less difficult, the road is far from easy. You will still have to put in real hours, and you will have to work hard. The point is that by establishing these good habits you won't have to work *as* hard. And when you do work, it won't seem so much like "work." And when you're done, you can actually *enjoy yourself!* More than that, you can enjoy yourself without guilt or that nagging sense when blowing off this class or that project that you're getting further and further into trouble.

The Essential Habits

Here is an overview of the essential habits in this book. Consistent with its theme (and with being a good student), if you're already highly proficient with a particular habit, skip to the next one. This is a book written for students who have a lot to do—futures to plan, parties to attend, résumés and cover letters to be mail-merged, experiences to be experienced—and only a few short years in which to do it all.

One important aspect of learning is repetition. My take on repetition is that it's best without unnecessary fluff. So, scan this list to keep these points in mind. Then let's dive in!

1. Make Your Study Efficient and Effective

2. Set Goals and Follow Up

3. Write Everyday

4. Be Active in Class

5. Study your Professor

6. Read Effectively

7. Break the Note-Taking Habit

8. Write your Own Outlines

9. Add to Your Outlines Daily

10. Plan One Day Per Week to Review for Each Final

11. Stay Organized

12. Make a Plan and Stick to It

13. Use University Resources

14. Work Now, Play Later

15. Keep Living Life

16. Maintain a Positive Attitude

Your First Week

These good habits should be goals you aim to achieve throughout your years as a student, but, for our purposes, the focus is immediate: what will you implement *for your first week of college?*

These habits are designed to make you a better college student, and you cannot afford to get behind. If, like most new college students, you wait until you "get it" to worry about your studies and habits, you'll see half the semester behind you—and midterms smack in front of you! Good habits in your very first week will put you in better shape for your entire college experience—and thus for your future. When you have good grades, you won't be afraid that your grades will negatively affect interviews with prospective employers or ruin graduate school chances. Good habits will help, big time. And the earlier you start, the better you will do and the more time you will have to actually enjoy yourself.

Poor habits, on the other hand, will not just hurt you early in your very first semester, but the effects of bad habits will continue to get bigger and bigger, threatening to steamroll right over you. These bad effects not only get bigger as your classes get more difficult, but they get worse: with bad habits you'll feel helpless in trying to catch up. Your dreams and aspirations will look increasingly less attainable—and then the negativity looms. For some, you'll start to think about giving up—and even *thinking* that becomes a dangerous, self-fulfilling prophecy. It happens far more often than it should.

If you implement these habits, now, then in addition to your successes in each course you will have a more positive experience in college, with more time and better (and easier) long-term success. Thus, let's focus on building the right habits, right up front. When? Right now, for your very first week.

Goals and Real Goals

As a college student, your goals should include not only doing well in your classes (*i.e.,* getting great grades), but also actually learning in each class what you're supposed to learn. In other words, you want to do well in college, but you also want to prepare yourself for later classes and for the real world.

This is not just cheerful academic-talk. It is important. Cramming might get you an "A-" or even an "A" on an exam—maybe—but it almost certainly won't help later. With cramming, you're lucky to remember ten concepts from your entire course. What a waste! With a better, more careful, more disciplined approach, you *won't have to* cram (which means you'll be able to relax at least a little before the exam), and you'll actually *understand* what it was that you were in class to learn. This will not only help you in later classes, but it will show when interviewing for your first job—and it will definitely show when you're actually working in your first job. It's one thing to fake out a professor or teaching assistant on an exam; it's another thing entirely to do so for four years (college), or for forty (your entire working life). As Lincoln's saying goes, you cannot fool all of the people all of the time.

INPUT AND OUTPUT, OR WORK AND GRADES

The advice in this book comes from personal experience. I want to impart what I learned about being a student: what worked and what did not. When I was in high school, for example, I quickly found that I had to do only the most minimal work for good grades in most classes. I would do homework assignments in a rush before class, and, well, very little else. Before each test I would crack open the text, cram a bit, and almost without fail would pass the class with flying colors. Chances are, if you're like most college-bound students, the same is true for you.

When I got to college, I found that things were different—very different. In most classes, there were a few assignments sprinkled throughout the semester, but the assignments were left almost completely up to us, the students, who thus had to be self-motivated enough to actually do them. After such bad habits in high school—which worked then—it was *very* hard to motivate and discipline myself to actually complete the weekly work. It was *so* much easier to let it slide, and have fun instead.

I mistakenly believed that these assignments were like those in high school, something that I could just make happen. I more or less just assumed I could "crank out" a paper quickly the day before it was due, just as I had always done. What happened instead were several horrible experiences—all-nighters when I realized that I didn't even know what the assignment was asking me to do. And since I hadn't really been paying attention in class, the professor's expectations were catching me by surprise. This was not something one could simply do in a rush—or at least not well. The following morning—the due date—was *not* the time to go to a professor with an absurdly basic question that would make it obvious I hadn't even *started*. Several times I turned in incomplete work. Other times, I *knew* that what I was handing in was just plain bad—or at best far below what it should have been. This was an awful feeling and a real wake-up call for me.

The same was true with my first-semester final exams. I figured that if I showed up to class, then I wouldn't have a problem on the exam. Sometimes yes, sometimes no. And even when I did okay, the truth is that I didn't really earn the grades I was given. With these experiences, I knew something was wrong. I knew I needed to change.

In trying to skate, I was wrong—and you will be too. College is different from high school in that it requires more. It also puts a much higher burden on students to manage their own time and efforts. Those higher standards are also what separate those with college degrees from those without.

One Step At a Time

In the following chapters, I will point out better ways to study and methods of self-motivation (and how to get over barriers of procrastination and inattention)—ultimately, I will show you how to do well in college. There is no magic formula for success: it takes implementing basic habits that can be applied to any learning style. These are habits that, when implemented correctly, will guide your educational experience in a positive direction without you having to think about it.

I am not here to outline everything you should expect from your college experience, as I am a supporter of experiencing life rather than reading about experiencing life. The purpose of this book is to give you the short, sweet, condensed version of what you need to know to succeed. It's short because soon you will be asked to read and understand mountains of projects and assignments. My job is to point out the habits you need to succeed—advice that would have helped me before and during my first year. When you are aware of the habits you need to develop, it is easier to take steps in that direction. It isn't an overnight change, but you can start right now at creating your own success in college. While the focus starts in your very first week, the benefits will extend far beyond then.

So please accept this book with its purpose and spirit in mind. As of this writing, I am finishing up law school, squeezing in a few minutes here and there for writing this. I did well in college— extremely well, in fact—and then again in law school, but that's as much confirmation of the value of these habits as it is a basis for any personal conceit. So, this is from one student to another: Advice from a grad-student who has not only been there and done that, but who is also right here along with you.

The Most Important Habit

The focus of this book is to develop one general habit that will not only help you be a stellar college student, but also help you throughout your working and personal life. This habit will put you a cut above most students and even most people you will ever encounter—and it seems like such a logical habit to develop. You'd think everyone would be focused on it, but for some reason we, maybe even as a species, just love to waste time.

Students spend a *lot* of time doing things they think are important and still more time doing things—be honest—they know aren't really all that important. Either way, this is simply wasting time. Much of this book is devoted to the number-one, most important overarching habit, which happens to include four parts:

1. Identifying things that waste time.

2. Refraining from doing things that waste time.

3. Identifying things that are both effective in learning and an efficient use of your time.

4. Doing more of those things in #3.

HABIT #1: MAKE YOUR STUDY EFFICIENT AND EFFECTIVE

This means you do what you must do to be the best student possible...and nothing more. This means that when you sit down to study, even if for short periods of time, you are getting the most from your time studying. If you can master this one principle and make it habitual, you will be successful. It *seems* easy, but as we all know, that doesn't necessarily *make* it easy.

We live in a time where it is possible to be extremely efficient. Possible. Not probable. We all have gadgets to keep us connected with the world around us, and these gadgets can be used to make learning easier. This may seem weird to those of you reading this, but I remember the advent of the computer and the internet—not all that long ago—and saw specifically how learning and access to information became easier and easier. I remember trying to do research projects in high school and not really knowing how to use the internet to study. I remember turning to the libraries and being bogged down with the amount of available information and no easy way to sift through the wealth of information in libraries. And then, as the internet became more accessible and easy to use, and as credible websites with the same vast wealth of information that existed in libraries started to pop up, the research and learning processes became easier and much, much more efficient. Along with the internet came more powerful computers and software that allowed the student to excel without wasting time. No longer do we have to sift through mountains of books at the library, nor are we restricted to taking hand-written notes. We can easily type papers and edit them with word processors—and the tools only seem to expand with each new device.

Here's an amusing assignment: ask a parent about writing papers on an actual typewriter. Then ask a grandparent about writing papers on a *manual* typewriter. This might be an eye-opener, as you realize that something we take for granted now—something as simple as centering text—used to be an annoying and time-consuming task, requiring counting the number of characters in each line to be centered, setting the typewriter to the center, and then counting backwards, manually, for one-half of those characters. For each line! Any mistakes? The *entire sheet* had to be redone.

This is an incredible time to be a student; efficiency is within our grasp! All it takes is a habit—a way of doing things that is reinforced by practice every day—to actually *be* efficient. And keep in mind what this means: being efficient means having *more* time to do what you would like to do, aside from learning whatever subject you're studying. This book is not about denial. It's about the opposite: learning well and quickly, preserving other time to relax without regret.

I won't spend more time now (which would be inefficient!), because much of what follows will be exactly this: developing the right habits to become more efficient and effective. But keep this overarching habit in mind as well. **Efficient, effective** study is the end goal, the most important goal, the crucial goal, the goal that will carry you through undergraduate successes and into your future successes. Effective and efficient study is the goal, the aim, and the most important habit you can develop in college.

2

Be Decisive and Set Goals

The first step to being decisive is finishing what you start. When you start school, finish it. When you start a semester, finish it. When you start an assignment, finish it. Do not waste your time with school if it isn't what you want to do—and the same goes for those who want to be in school but who fritter away their time instead. So, the first lesson is this: finish what you start. If you're not going to finish, then don't bother starting.

Here's why: life goes forward whether you are working toward your future or not. Whether you like it or not, or are prepared or not, you will grow up—or at least you will grow older—and as time marches on, you will find yourself married or in serious relationships, wanting children, wanting cars, wanting a house or a condo, wanting to travel, and wanting *things* in general. You will need these things too, as those who provided them throughout your early life become less and less willing to shell out *their* hard-earned cash to pay for their grown kid's food and expenses. Sure, you could always just wait for the parental units to keel over and then receive that nice inheritance—but that would be out of line with the efficient and self-actualized and success-oriented themes of this book. (And it's not a terribly nice sentiment anyway.)

The point is, life doesn't stop moving. If you want something in your future you've got to make a decision *now,* and move toward that goal. The longer you wait, the harder it gets. I know several friends who waffled and procrastinated their decisions about school and careers and eventually found themselves painted into a corner. One friend of mine is married with children, needs the extra income that comes with experience on a job or a college degree, but *still* hasn't decided what to do. His ability to move forward is now increasingly burdened with day-to-day financial and family obligations. Instead of working toward something that he really wants out of life, he is forced to work three jobs just to get by. He painted himself into a corner by not making a decision and moving forward. Even a decision that was just partially right would have been better than no decision at all, as chances are he could have then moved from a partially good career to another one more in line with his true preferences.

MAJORS

The same goes for those who fritter away time trying to grasp their long-term goals or even "decide on a major." They take class after class—with no real, cohesive plan—and put off the inevitable decision. They are ultimately wasting time—and they aren't generally having that much fun in their meandering classes. (And they certainly won't have fun when they finally *are* forced to declare a major and take all those hard courses at once.)

Learn from my mistake: as of my junior year, I hadn't chosen a major. If I had, I would have been nearly a year ahead of where I am right now in terms of education and career. And I'm not alone. Being undecided is almost a joke for many college students, in part because there *are* so many careers and paths to choose from, and many of us don't want to be "tied down" to anything in particular. As human beings, I think we *want* to be committed to something (which is why we go to college), but we have a hard time actually committing. So we bounce from one major to another and eventually become what is politely termed a "career student."

Among other issues, this costs more money—a lot more. Even if Mom and Dad are paying (which is hardly fair to them), this is more time, more headache, and when you do get to the end of your program, you're going to want it *to be over.* And, for goodness' sake, if you're going to still be in school, wouldn't it be smarter to spend that time and money instead in a graduate program, where rather than working sideways you'll at least be adding to your future?

While there might be some for whom a "career" as a student is right—perhaps by going back to school after they've made some money or have served in the Peace Corps or military—no one wants to be around (or hire) a career student when that is all there is. Take my word for it: after a while career students start to smell funny.

Okay then, what's the problem? You *know* the kinds of things you like—you really do. Think back to high school. It should be a good clue to you when you go into a class or open a book for a particular class and find yourself either cringing or at least half-way enjoying yourself. So, which is it? For those classes that you enjoy, narrow them down—try to picture yourself doing that for the rest of your life. Did you *like* history? Did you find yourself wondering about related subjects when you were studying, say, the Emancipation Proclamation? Can you picture yourself studying that for the rest of your life? Or, how about science? Did you find lab work really fascinating...or deadly boring? No matter what, you have just got to *make the decision*—and the sooner the better.

THE PERFECT AS THE ENEMY OF THE GOOD, OR WHY YOUR DECISION NEEDS TO BE ONLY MOSTLY RIGHT

One more point is worth mentioning: yours doesn't have to be the perfect decision. It just has to be a good decision.

If you liked history, let's say, and you decide to proceed down that path, in your first two years of college you'll be required to take a number of "lower-division" courses in a variety of fields—this is the interdisciplinary approach of a broad education, required by all colleges—plus also courses in a specific field that are prerequisite to higher courses in that field. So, let's say you remember your history courses fondly. You take a variety of other courses, plus one or two history courses each semester.

Now let's say you realize you really don't like history that much after all. You realize, after one of those other courses, that you really *love* geography! And not just any geography, but geography and sociology combined. You have not only just put yourself way ahead of the game, you have also *not* wasted any time. Why? Because those courses you took—the ones you realized you didn't love—they still count. They're still within your lower-division credit requirements. Chances are, if what you thought you loved is close to what you find you really love—because your decision was mostly right—some of those courses will even count for *upper*-division credit (*i.e.*, credits within your major). Life is good.

The same principle applies to all majors. Start in chemistry and realize you like physics? Same. Start in music and realize you love dance? Same. This even applies if you decide that you really love something completely outside what you originally thought: start in history and realize you love dance? As long as you learn this relatively early—such as in the first two or three semesters—same!

On a related topic, think about a minor as well. You don't have to love just one field. Within reason, a careful plan will get you a solid major plus a fun minor without additional work—the best of both worlds. If you're lucky, both will be fun. If not, you still need to decide.

And think also about the value you would bring to an employer. If you like languages, for example, taking a minor in at least one language is a *superb* decision. Even if you're *not* sure you like languages, you really should think about this. If you're looking for a job in chemistry and you also speak Chinese fluently (or Japanese or French or Spanish or even Latin), who do you think has the upper hand in interviews? You'd be surprised at how employers are interested in science majors who also minored in one of the liberal arts—or vice versa. And it works in any direction. A history major with minors in physics and French? That's just *interesting!* (And, believe it or not, with a careful approach you will get "double credit" for at least some of the courses, such as *French Pre-Renaissance Literary History* or *History of Science: Physicists in the Age of Discovery.*) It will almost certainly get you more and better conversations with potential employers—even if they're not otherwise looking for historians of science who also happen to be able to order lunch in French.

Consider your finances and timeframe, as well. I remember being strapped for cash one semester. I seriously thought about dropping out for a while to work. I proposed this idea to one of my mentors, a brilliant professor who perfectly matched the collegiate professor "look." He told me to suck it up and push through, because the value of graduating a semester earlier is much more than the value of working a "student" job for the same number of months. And this assumes you'll actually get back in to finish what you started. If you don't (which happens all too often), you'll be in the same situation as my friend who's stuck in dead-end jobs. The same principle applies to wasting time while trying to decide on your major. You may enjoy a few extra classes, throw a few extra parties, but ultimately, you will be further ahead if you just make a decision already!

My advice is this: think seriously about what you love. Think seriously about what you don't love. Connect those, and do whatever you have to do to decide what you want to study. Then make a decision *as soon as possible.* If it's even roughly correct, you'll still be miles ahead—and chances are what you learn in each new set of classes will help you to fine-tune your choice. Your early decisions will support your later ones.

BE DECISIVE

When I write "do whatever you have to do," I mean it. Every person is different and will approach the decision differently, but at the end of the day, it is a decision that you will have to make. I understand that the decision is hard; I've been there, not too long ago. But you will thank yourself after you do some serious, introspective thinking and decision-making. To mix metaphors, it's a dog-eat-dog world out there, and you need to be on your game with where your life's journey is headed. 'Cause if you're not constantly moving forward with your education and career, chances are you're moving sideways—or backwards. And those who have made their mostly-right decisions early will be at a great advantage compared to those who are eventually forced to decide.

Worse, not making a decision *is* a decision. But it's usually a mostly-wrong decision—such as later taking whatever major will get-you-out-with-the-least-amount-of-extra-coursework, or even dropping out entirely, never to finish. Even if you drop out to start the next Fortune 500 business, chances are you'll always look back with regret at what you never finished.

On a side-note: have you ever noticed that in college-themed horror movies, it is usually the slacker students who meet their demise early? This is for several reasons, of course: if the kid isn't doing anything, then there won't be any serious repercussions if he's knocked off first. On the other hand, kill the pretty pre-med heroine and all hell breaks loose as the cops scramble to figure out whodunit and nab the creep. The "right" sequence works on the technical, story development side too: we, the audience, relate more to people who have goals and are doing meaningful things with their lives. Why? Perhaps *we* want to be doing something meaningful with our lives. When the slacker dies, it is scary, sure, but when the person with a future dies, it is more sad than scary. If horror movies were sad, then they wouldn't be all that much fun—so you kill off the slacker students first for some early scares and then allow the audience to get attached to the student with a future. *Then* the movie has a chance. So, if you ever find yourself in a horror movie, your chances are much better if you have a future that you're actually working toward.

So be decisive. Don't get killed off.

Making decisions and sticking with them works hand-in-hand with our next habit: setting goals.

Habit #2: Set Goals and Follow Up

Goals are self-explanatory. If you set a goal, then you are in reality competing *with yourself* to accomplish that goal. If you compete honestly, you will be more successful than if you cut corners, and you will definitely be more successful than if you had never set a goal in the first place.

Setting goals will help you save time because you know both the end result you would like to see and what you have to do to get there. Setting goals also reduces the danger of procrastination, as it makes initial steps more concrete and logical, and thus easier. More time is obviously better, because this allows you to focus on actual studying. You can also relax a little more (and with less worry) than if you did not set goals (and thus didn't have the extra time that the goal-setting gave you).

Setting goals helps you be more productive because you are working towards something, and know what it is you are working towards. This seems obvious, but the common, bad habit of simply "studying" means that many students don't really know whether they're accomplishing a goal, because they never think of it *as* a goal.

Setting goals decreases your level of stress, especially when you can see progress. This you will see if you set reasonable goals. For example, don't say, "I will read and prepare every Saturday for all my classes for the following week!" Instead, try "I will prepare for each class for at least one hour the day before that class."

The first "goal" is just silly; there is no way you can accomplish that unreasonable objective every single Saturday, so you're setting yourself up for failure. It isn't that you will fail your classes, necessarily. No, you'll likely just fail to accomplish your goal. I write this from my own frustrated experience. Even if you do prepare a week in advance, what if the professor misses class or changes the schedule? It also happens that a time-intensive project will prevent you from accomplishing everything you had "planned"—trashing your hopes to get everything done at once.

Ultimately, an unrealistic goal simply won't work. It certainly won't work for an extended period—say, for an entire semester. With an unreasonable goal (or with no goal at all), you're going to be miserable *and* ineffective. The realistic, concrete goal is not just reasonable: it means that you're far more likely to actually finish all of your studying and assignments, far earlier than you would if you just "studied," *and* you're going to feel better along the way. You're going to see real progress every day!

I'm sorry to keep hammering away on this, but as we're early in the book with the most basic start, this is worth repeating: with an unreasonable goal (such as studying for all classes on one day), what is likely to happen is that you'll get bogged down—and then decide to blow it off because your friends are heading out for a night of fun and why shouldn't you have some fun too? You end up with the worst of both worlds, and if you don't spot and correct this pattern early, one Saturday will turn into a semester of blown chances—and you *still* have those final exams and research papers due. With reasonable goals set to take advantage of your best times in manageable bites, you can prepare before each class and tackle that research project. You'll do so with less fuss, *and* you'll accomplish your goal—getting good grades. No, let's make that getting *great* grades, earned with less effort and less worry than with frantic, inefficient, last-minute cramming.

In setting goals, you will eliminate annoying questions such as "What should I study today?" or "What should I be doing right at this moment?" With goals, you know what you need to be doing. Setting goals helps you focus and stay on track. You are a college student committed to being effective and efficient. You will develop habits to be a successful college student and to lay the groundwork for success in your career. You *stay* on this path towards success by setting goals.

HOW, SPECIFICALLY

You want to get in the habit of setting short-term, attainable goals. You should also have longer-term goals, of course: doing well on your exams, getting an amazing internship or summer job, getting into a great graduate school, and pursuing your dream career. All of these are good, and you should keep all in mind. But these are not *day-to-day* goals. Your main focus, especially in your first year of college, should be on what you do each day of each week. A "focus" doesn't mean a rigid, death-grip schedule. It means simply planning and knowing. This takes mere minutes, if not seconds. Planning saves time, and knowing doesn't take any time at all—it takes attention.

As you progress through college, your focus will gradually broaden. For example, when you first get to college, you will want to focus on getting good grades in your first courses especially. As discussed, the world of college can be a shock when coming from high school, and a bit of extra focus at the beginning—*your* beginning—is crucial. Why? Among other reasons, great grades to start will give you breathing room with regard to scheduling and other academic and career options. Poor grades, on the other hand, will be like a dead weight: it takes *enormous* effort to try to bring up a GPA once it's already down—and for some graduate programs it simply won't work. It's important to remember that the "A" part of GPA stands for "Average," which means that it takes a *lot* of individual effort to change a collection of grades. You've heard of a "moving average"? They're used to smooth a set of data points, so as to give a better, more focused picture. They also, by definition, move much more slowly than those data points. The more grades you have, the harder it is to move that average. Also, consider that your early courses are *easy* compared with the upper-level courses you'll need to take in your major.

As you gather a bit more experience in college, as well as apply the habits in this book, you will find that it becomes easier to be effective, to know what your professor is looking for, and thus to get those high grades. So, right from the beginning and through your first year, you will want to set goals that lead toward reinforcing good habits and earning good grades. In your second year, if you haven't picked a major or decided on a career path, you will want to focus your goals on making those decisions (again, as soon as possible), as well as landing internships or beefing up your résumé with community service, extra-curricular activities, etc.

During your last two years, you will be focused on your actual major and on the imminent end to your undergraduate career and what follows from there. I decided on law school, for example, so that involved taking the LSAT, researching numerous law schools, and preparing applications. Each of these took a lot of time—and, because law schools are just as concerned with final grades, I couldn't let up in my actual course work just because I was nearly done.

This process will be similar for anyone who chooses to continue their education and even for those who jump right into their careers. Even if you aren't interested in graduate school, or at least not immediately, you will still need to decide on an industry or type of work, research places to work, and prepare for a seemingly endless round of résumés and interviews. You will need to send out job applications, attend career fairs and networking events, buy new interview clothes, and sweat through the actual interviews—all while keeping your grades up during your last two years.

If you wait until you are done or nearly done with college before preparing for either graduate school or employment, you are almost certainly headed for a nightmare. Unless your extended family includes a senator or CEO who is willing to vouch for your dedication (when, *ahem,* you've just shown the opposite), you will be wasting time and the valuable asset you've just earned—your undergraduate degree. A better result just takes planning: setting realistic goals, and then working towards those goals. (If your aunt or uncle *is* a senator or CEO, chances are they're *expert* at setting goals and then working toward those goals. If you want to shine in their light, it helps to put the batteries in.)

I made a goal, for example, to review my class notes within a few hours after each class, and to incorporate them into my final study notes (a concept that we will discuss shortly). The goal was a general one that applied to all of my classes. It was something I could follow up with each day, and see progress. I retained more information on the days I reviewed my notes and added the few important lines to my final study notes than on the days I did not. Not only did I notice the difference, but this goal also helped me be more effective every day. But it didn't stop there. Reviewing class notes, along with other short-term goals, leads to success in your long-term goals. Because I had made this goal to review my class notes early on, I didn't have to waste time *re-learning* the material or cramming for finals. I became a more efficient student, which opened the doors to opportunities and to other good habits... which further reinforced this positive cycle. (Among other things, I later had time to excel in law school *and* write two books.)

So, don't think of short-term goals and long-term goals as opposites. Short-term goals pave the way for long-term goals, and long-term goals help define (and redefine) those short-term goals. Keep your long-term goals in mind while you focus on simple, immediate, achievable goals. Goals are about making progress, so make your goals *possible*. Pick a few goals to start out with, master those, and then add more.

As you can see, part of your goal-setting involves striking a balance between getting good grades and getting the most out of college (and having some fun), while preparing for the future. This balance is one of the most difficult things you will have to deal with in college—and it doesn't stop there. The challenge continues on through your life. Just the other day, I was speaking with a partner at the law firm in which I work. (A partner is the "boss" in a law firm. So, for the first ten years of practice, a new lawyer will have many bosses.) This partner was extremely busy, his desk piled high with reports, legal documents, and client information. He seemed to be working a million miles a minute, answering phone calls, sending emails, changing direction seemingly every minute. I asked him if this was normal, and he smiled. He said that the trick to being a good lawyer is the ability to juggle multiple endeavors, well, all at once.

The same balancing act applies to virtually any field you could possibly enter. Okay, if you go to a remote forest to study orang-utans, your focus might be slightly narrower. But then again, you *will* have to juggle actual *survival*—so maybe it isn't that different after all.

So, set goals *now.* Set goals you can achieve immediately and every day. Those achievable and consistent goals will in turn allow you to balance everything you have to do, and help you set longer-term, overarching goals.

Follow-Up

The most important part of setting goals is not just the goal itself. Yes, you read that right. The most important part of setting goals is not just the goal itself, *but the follow-up.*

If you do not follow up, you're not really working toward that goal...chances are you're doing more dreaming than actual work. At the very least, failing to follow up means that you don't know whether you're reaching your goal—which means that you won't know whether that goal is the right goal and whether the next goal will ever follow. A goal is about checking your progress and seeing your improvement. In other words, *following up:* what was the goal? Was it met? Was it the right goal? Was your learning both effective and efficient? Will it help you for final exams? Will the goal help you in your future? What should be your next goal?

One way to see your progress is to keep a running record of your goals and assess how well you are progressing. Set aside a brief period each week to follow up on your goals and to fine-tune your next goals. It doesn't take an afternoon. It doesn't even take an hour. Once you make this a habit, it can be done in minutes—and each new goal will be better and more easily tracked the following week.

Once your goals become habits, set more goals. Make your time as a college student better and more effective. Continue to do this—

make a habit of making goals and following up—and you will find more success in every aspect of what you do, and ultimately you will have a more balanced, more enjoyable life.

I can almost hear what you're thinking:

"This is too much work!"

"You're trying to make me into a robot!!"

"This will take all the spontaneity and fun out of life!!!"

No it's not, no I'm not, and no it won't. Not only can you still have fun, you can actually have more fun, with less overall work, because you'll get your work done quickly, you won't feel guilty when you're not working, and you won't be stressed when final exams do come around. Sure, you can be spontaneous. But *all the time?* That doesn't sound like anyone successful I've known—and those who *are* successful are not robots. Focused, sure. But they're less likely to be robotic than, say, the person who's been playing video games for two days straight.

3

WRITING WELL

I have been through nearly seven years of post-secondary and professional education, and I have taken many classes on many different subjects. Still, people look at me a bit funny when I tell them that the courses I learned the most from, or those that helped me more than others, were a class on typing and the several I've taken through the years on writing.

It might help to remember that I entered high school just as computers were becoming more popular and more accessible—so a class on typing was great because with what limited experience I had with computers, I learned to type quickly and efficiently. Most of us do so now because we use keyboards so much—but that doesn't mean we do so efficiently. And who knows? In a few years there might be a new interface entirely—maybe a direct neural connection—and then *you'll* be the old fogey with old-fashioned skills. (Yes, they'll look at you in disbelief: "You actually typed with your *fingers!?!*")

HABIT #3: WRITE EVERYDAY

Writing, on the other hand, is not something you pick up while on a social-networking page, cell phone, or any other typing-related activity. Writing is a craft—a skill that needs to be learned and practiced—and it's also part of what you do with your mind.

Learning to write well means that you have to learn technical rules, like grammar and punctuation; structural rules, such as thesis statements, topic sentences, and transitions; and most importantly, conceptual ideas. Writing involves accurately portraying your thoughts on paper in such a way that your thoughts are conveyed clearly to the reader. The reader, who is not you, must be able to understand what it is you're writing. And when the situation calls for it, your reader (who might just disagree with you) must be persuaded that you are right. This is a skill that is lacking in the United States today—it doesn't take much of a curmudgeon to admit that our grandparents could out-write us cold. Just because we have new tools doesn't mean we don't also need to know how to use them. You will be that much further ahead if you learn how.

So why is writing so important? After all, there are many jobs that seem not to require writing skills, right?

The answer is a resounding…*"Wrong."*

There are obvious careers that involve a large amount of writing. Some careers (like law, journalism, teaching, government) require writing as a fundamental part of each day. Even in "non-writing" careers such as in business, no manager gets by without knowing how to write well and concisely. Writing concisely is harder than writing a whole bunch of words to say the same thing, and managers are extremely sensitive to wasting time—especially if it's a subordinate who's wasting their time.

What about the really non-writing careers, such as science and engineering? How about a test? Go to the nearest scientist or engineer and ask them whether they need to know how to write. Chances are their writing is quite different—even more condensed and specialized than for the business manager. But there's no way they're going to be successful if they cannot write. Even a computer programmer is an *expert* at writing—it's just in a different language.

It should go without saying that you will need to know how to write—and write *well*—in college. You will be required to write research papers and topical reports and lab results and quizzes and exams and any of a number of other assignments. Can you hide and scurry around the hard courses? Well, yes you can, at least somewhat. But you'll be doing yourself no favors, because you'll *need* those skills even more after college. And if you try to get into graduate school after four years of remedial underwater basket-weaving, well, good luck. Those admissions committees aren't snobbish because they're academic snobs—or at least not *just* because they're academic snobs. They really *are* looking for skill. Among those skills is the ability to communicate, to use the currency that is one of the committee member's most prized: the English language.

Besides your future endeavors as a student and those obvious examples of careers requiring strong writing skills, practically any career or educational path you choose will include writing in one way or another.

To illustrate, let's go even farther afield to careers we wouldn't assume to involve writing. Take studying orangutans in the middle of somewhere, hundreds of miles from the nearest city. You're outside of civilization, so what's the need to be civilized? Well, much of your time will be recording your thoughts and observations—which, you guessed it, includes writing. Looking at this from a larger perspective, assuming you make it out of the jungle alive, you will probably want to publish your findings, or at least make others aware of what you've been doing all that time near orangutans. Maybe you'd like a research grant? Maybe you'd like to complete a doctorate in animal research? Maybe you'd like to get hired by a university?

This is the same for every field in the sciences, because scientists are professional observers—and observations will need to be recorded. It also applies in careers that involve an abundant use of math: Findings will have to be communicated, most often through a writing of some kind. Even trade-based careers like plumbing involve writing. (I realize that if you are reading this book, you are probably not going into a trade, but rather are going into a career that stems from a college education. But if you're hiring a plumber, you might want to know that he can read the emergency instructions on your new water heater.) In plumbing and other trades, there are reports and records to be kept with each visit, which requires writing. Poor records mean that you might re-pay for something that was already done, or not have something done that needs to be done.

Aside from making reports and keeping records, another reason that writing skills are so important is email. Email is the number one form of communication (at least for now), and despite the seeming informalities of this form of communication, it requires at least rudimentary skill. A lack of skill is immediately apparent. Your writing is often the first impression that you give to others. Be it an article that you want published or a "quick" note to a boss or future employer, readers will look at what you've written and they *will* judge you. They will pinpoint any grammatical mistakes or sentences that don't make sense. Your writing is a banner that advertises you, for better or for worse.

To further illustrate this point (and, yes, I know I'm nagging), consider the following summary from a College Board study.

> Writing is a "threshold skill" for both employment and promotion, particularly for salaried employees [such as college graduates]. Half the responding companies report that they take writing into consideration when hiring professional employees.
>
> "In most cases, writing ability could be your ticket in…or it could be your ticket out," said one respondent.
>
> A similar dynamic is at work during promotions. Half of all companies take writing into account when making promotion decisions. One succinct comment: "You can't move up without writing skills."
>
> People who cannot write and communicate clearly will not be hired and are unlikely to last long enough to be considered for promotion.
>
> "Poorly written application materials would be extremely prejudicial," said one respondent. "Such applicants would not be considered for any position."

As part of my experience as a law clerk, I had the opportunity to comb through thousands of pages of correspondence among and to attorneys, CEOs, and other individuals in high-profile positions. You wouldn't believe the volume of errors, or emails that made absolutely no sense whatsoever. It makes a *huge* difference when you read an email that is well written. I also had the opportunity to work with a professor in college, grading papers. You can tell almost instantly which writers are competent and which are not. I was amazed. *One hundred percent of the time,* those who can organize and articulate their thoughts well on paper, whether the arguments themselves are good or completely off base, will get a better grade. And, more often than not, someone who knows how to write well also knows when an argument is solid or specious—so it's not likely a good writer is completely off base.

The ability to write well is part of success. Thus, make this a central goal for your first year of college.

Implementing the Habit Of Good Writing

Okay, we know that writing is important. How do we get to the point where *your* writing is not just good enough, but authoritative and convincing?

One of the first things you should do is to enroll yourself into a writing class as soon as you can—preferably in your very first semester in college. You'll need the course anyway, so why not now? If you can qualify for and take an honors English course, do so. Challenge yourself! Seek out what's hard, not just what's easy. English will add to the foundation from high school and provide the opportunity to practice writing on an academic, collegiate level. It will also help you to build your writing endurance, as you will soon have to write papers and reports much longer than you are used to.

If, by the way, you're still in high school and haven't yet had an advanced English course—drop another class and add a writing one. The hardest one you can get. An Advanced Placement course if you can. Your first-year courses in college are usually ones that you can take throughout your years at school, but they're designed to be taken early. So get English out of the way—and get it into your mind, before you have substantive courses in your major to worry about.

Another goal you can set in developing a habit of good writing is to read critically and write something every day. Reading "critically" does not mean being negative—although that's often how it's perceived. Reading *critically* means to understand why something is stated as it is and to challenge whether that is correct. Stephen King, the prolific novelist, has written quite a lot about writing. Among his assertions, King declares that if you want to be good at writing, then set aside four hours to read and write, every day. Other writers have compared writing to practicing sports or a musical instrument as a profession—it must be done, every day, if you want to be good.

Now, most of us are probably not working toward becoming novelists, but the principle rings true. If you want to be good at something, really good, you have to actually do it. It takes practice. To be a good writer—which is *essential* in school *and* in your future career—you must work at it every day.

Reading critically is almost as important as writing, and it does not really matter what you are reading, as long as you are paying attention—real attention—to how it is written. It could be the newspaper, online news articles, novels, or virtually anything else. Pay attention to sentence structure and word choice. As you read, ask yourself if you would have worded a paragraph differently, or organized the writing in a more cohesive manner, or flat out taken a different stance from what is written. Even if you agree with what you read, ask yourself what assumptions the writer is making. (Writers make *lots* of assumptions. Some valid, some not.) Look at what the author did well and place those techniques and styles in a bank in your mind to test and implement in your own writing. Pay attention to the writing flow—what makes it effective for the reader or the flaw that kills the piece. By reading, your writing will come more naturally as your brain will be more used to words (and more used to *more* words), and what you can do with them.

As with reading, you need to write something every day—at least a paragraph or two. Write in your journal; get started on your project draft; get back to editing a different assignment; write a letter to the editor, to a friend, to your congressman; start a novel; just *write*. As you do this, you will not only implement the skills learned in writing classes, but you will also train your mind to put your thoughts on paper. The more you write, the better you'll get. Your habit of critical reading will come into play as you start to notice good and bad techniques in your *own* writing, thereby making it easier for you to improve.

Not only will this practice pay off in the long run when you are asked to present a presentation to a group of coworkers or write a 300-page dissertation, but it will also pay off in the immediate sense that writing papers and assignments will become easier. No longer will you have to toil over every word and sentence—the writing will come because you've already developed your mind and its facility in language.

The bottom line is this: learn how to write well, and then keep learning. Make it a habit, and work on refining your skill. If that means spending an extra hour in double-checking rules of punctuation and grammar for each assignment in your first year (and, yes, that is what it means), then that's what you do. This is not the place to "save" time. Building knowledge and skill—*that* will save time. And it will save time when it counts, such as in an exam.

There is no "end" in good writing; there is always room for improvement. And virtually everything you write in college and later in your career will be improved as you focus on writing. You will most certainly thank yourself later if you work at this sooner.

4

EFFECTIVE CLASS TIME

So you get to class on your first day. You'll see many of your future classmates sitting around, mostly toward the back of the room. The feeling of anxiety will weigh heavily in the room. Some of your fellow students might already be reviewing their textbooks while others are typing away at their computers, but most are sitting quietly, nervously, waiting for the professor to arrive. Everyone is tense; no one quite knows what to do.

It's a weird sensation because every single person in that room has been through years of schooling where they have developed skills and habits in many different classrooms—yet the first day of college is somehow different. Maybe it is because college is such an important step in securing a successful future, maybe we're nervous because it is so expensive and different, or maybe it is just because we are programmed to be nervous on the first day of *any* school.

DON'T BE NERVOUS

You shouldn't be nervous, because you're going to know many of your classmates pretty well before it's all over. After a few weeks, that nervousness will disappear, and you'll realize that everyone there is just like you and that there was no reason for all that anxiety. But saying that won't change how you are going to feel, so use your nervousness. Let it help keep you alert.

Take a deep breath, and, if seating is not assigned in your class, then *choose* where you're going to sit. Although the task of finding a place to sit might seem insignificant, it will affect the rest of your time in that classroom. Many try to stay near the back of the room, hoping that the professor won't notice them.

I've got a secret for you. People who sit in the back, or otherwise try to "hide" in the classroom, can get called on more. It's not as if professors aren't aware of what's what. They've caught on to this tactic and will seek out those who try to hide—and when they don't, it's not because they don't understand, but because they've written that row off.

After years of sitting in the back row through much of my undergraduate years, I made up my mind for law school that I would sit in the front. I spent the entire first year as the only student sitting in the front row in most of my classes. Call me a dork, brown-noser, whatever, but professors acknowledged me as the only student in the front row, and after that...they went after those behind me. Unless I raised my hand, I received hardly any attention at all. I wish I had realized this back in college.

And, no, you don't want to have your hand constantly raised. In law school this is called "gunning," and it's a *very* bad habit. It's annoying to professors, you will learn less, and it will guarantee you a minimum of friends.

Sitting in the front row was good for me in other ways. First, it is hard *not* to pay attention when you are up front. No matter how tired you might be, you are hardly ever tempted to fall asleep with the professor only a few feet away. Second, you are not distracted by others who would be sitting in front of you if you were further back. Third, you would think that with the kind of money we spend to go to college, everyone would be in rapt attention during class. But—surprise, surprise—this is simply not the case. Tying into the second reason, if you sit anywhere in the classroom except the front row, you will see students using their computers for just about everything *but* your class: surfing the web, messaging, and playing games. Even if you don't want to be distracted, these are real distractions: the guy in front of you checking on scores for March Madness or—no joke—the girl in front of you buying holiday lingerie. Needless to say, these make it rather hard to concentrate.

Sitting in the front row was one of the best decisions I made in law school, and it's one I wish I had made in college. It really did help. That written, you've got to do what's right for you. After all, if *you're* the one checking scores or buying lingerie, there's not a person behind you who won't know it.

Also, your personality plays into this. I ended up being the only one in the front row in many of my classes, and there were times when I was a little lonely. But, because it was law school and

I had a family to think about, I made the decision seriously. It was akin to a business decision. This didn't mean I didn't care about being friendly—just not during class time. While the front row helped me stay active and attentive in class, I reserved time *after* class to chat and be friendly. No one seemed to be put off.

Don't forget what this is all about: being active and attentive. This leads us to Habit Number Four.

HABIT #4: BE ACTIVE IN CLASS

Before we get started, it is important to go over where your grade comes from in college. In high school, brownie points might have made a difference. In college, your grade will often be a culmination of assignments and usually two exams: a midterm exam and a final exam. There can be quizzes or perhaps a research paper, and there will likely be a component for participation. You should not participate in class only for the sake of brown-nosing, however. The age-old dislike of people who kiss up to their professors is the same in college as it ever was—and it's apparent to everyone, including the professor. No, you are active in class so you can get the most out of it, and as a result of actually getting the most out of it, you will get a higher grade.

It is thus important to remember that your activity in class is a means to an end. The "end" is the final exam. The real end is actually learning the subject. There are no brownie points for brown-nosing. In other words, stay active in class not for those relatively minor participation points (if any), but as a way to gauge and boost your progress and *learn* from your professor. Everything you do in class should lead to success on the final exam; the final exam is "only" an indication of what you actually learn.

But it gets better! In additional to all that, something magical will happen: the more you focus on the practical aspects of your classes, the more likely you'll actually start to *enjoy* your time. After all, what fun is it to think only about partying, messaging, and anything-but-classwork if you have to force yourself to tolerate those miserable classes? Why not enjoy them both? With better planning and a better attitude, you can. *And* you can set yourself up for career success while actually enjoying yourself.

College should be fun. All of it.

SPECIFICALLY...

What does being active in class actually mean?

To be active in class might mean different things for different people. For me (after I learned better) it was sitting in front and participating occasionally in the class discussion. I found that I was most active when I expressed my opinion about what we were studying in the class, asking questions or making comments about points that were bothering me. I got *much* more out of the class and was able to follow the lecture when I participated—and I did not "zone out" as I did when I sat in the back and played the cool renegade. Participation helps too with thoroughness, avoiding procrastination, and overall motivation.

Here's an important point: this type of "being active" should not mean "be a gunner." A *gunner* is a person who talks excessively, who spouts opinion after opinion, and who is an all-around unpleasant addition to (or should I say subtraction from) the class. It doesn't take many class sessions before *everyone* knows—and avoids—the gunners. Even if you like to talk, do not be a gunner. Pace yourself. Comment only when you *truly* have something important to say—which shouldn't be that often, really. You're there to learn, not to teach...and especially not to preach.

This is a spectrum, of course, so be careful. If you are shy, give yourself a challenge: talk a little. If you love to talk, give yourself a challenge: try *not* to talk so much in class—save it for outside bull sessions with the appropriate group. Remember, too, that gunners aren't getting an "A" simply by talking and talking and talking. Talk is cheap in college; an "A" is not. Even professors get annoyed by gunning and obvious brown-nosing, so don't think that you'll get automatic points just 'cause.

I had a classmate who took the whole "class participation" thing *way* too seriously. He made comments about everything to the point where the rest of us were absolutely sick of hearing his voice. Even our professors got noticeably tired of his constant remarks and opinions. And, even though he annoyed us to no end, sometimes he made good comments and had some fairly interesting insights. I found myself jotting down things he said because they made sense. Sometimes those notes helped, but more often they were a source of confusion—primarily because after a few weeks I forgot who'd said whatever it was that I had written down. I didn't know whether the comment was from the professor or from another student. If it was from the professor, then I needed to remember it; otherwise, no way. So, the rule of thumb should be to pay attention to your *professor.* Listen to the lectures and to responses in discussions, and take note of *only what the professor says.*

Professors will emphasize what they think is important, so do not be worried about missing a comment from a classmate. One professor would listen to comments and then politely move on with the lecture. She would answer questions, but mainly stuck to her plan. This was a nice way of her saying, "You need to understand what *I* am saying. I don't mind good discussion, but don't mistake that for what *I'm* discussing."

Remember during these class discussions that it is your professor giving the exams, and so it is what your professor thinks is important that *is* important. And, it is the professor who has studied in this field for years, perhaps decades. Consequently, that's the person you need to pay attention to.

LISTEN. REALLY LISTEN.

An important part of being active in class is, of course, to prepare before each class. This means to read what you were supposed to have read. The second part of this is to *listen.* This word, "listen," doesn't mean simply *hear.* It means to *engage,* mentally, with the discussion.

Listen *intently* to what your professor is saying. This means you are actively listening and trying to comprehend your professor. You are mentally challenging the professor's statements and explanations, and engaging in a silent *dialogue.* This seems to be a concept almost not worth mentioning—after all, who's going to say they're not going to listen to the professor?—but you'd be surprised by all of those web surfers and lingerie shoppers. And even those who seem to be listening…aren't really. They're wandering, daydreaming, thinking about surfing the web or buying lingerie. Stop. Your mental time is valuable. As long as you're there, use it. Listen. Really listen.

This brings us to the next important habit.

Habit #5: Study Your Professor

Your professor will give you some valuable insight into what he or she is looking for on an exam. In fact, I would argue that studying your professor is an integral part of success in college. Of course, you want to stay current in your reading and ultimately you want to learn the subject of your class—but your professor's assignments and exams are the immediate hurdle, and you pass them by knowing *exactly* what the professor expects. Yet how can you know exactly? This is shockingly easy. But not all students think about their courses in such a way as to understand just how logical it is.

Every professor wants something different—but they're all working toward a similar goal. That goal is not to "teach" you, even if that's what they're getting paid to do. Their real goal is to convey the deeper meaning of the subject; their allegiance (if you're lucky) is to their profession, not you. This is important in two ways. First, do not treat them like service providers. They *hate* that (for good reason), and it will backfire. They do not owe you a grade, and they do not owe you some slack when you forget to finish your assignment. Second, stop trying to build the entire relationship on brown-nosing; instead, focus on actually absorbing the subject that is their passion. *That* will make them your ally.

Okay, let's get back to the classroom: some professors like the details, while others prefer the general concepts. Some like it when their words are repeated verbatim in an answer on an exam, while others give the highest grades for independent thought and analysis. How the professor conducts class time is a good indication of how to do well on the exam.

I had a professor, for example, who would parse the language of philosophical theories. She used the comments from the textbook as a springboard for discussion about theoretical interpretation. (Much of philosophy is in comparing comments and responses of other philosophers to particular theories.) On the exam, I did extremely well by doing what she did in class. I took apart the theories, line by line and sometimes even word by word, and analyzed differing interpretations. I followed her classroom example and didn't include all the other textbook filler in the exam. Other philosophy professors might insist that the current consensus or other commentary on philosophical theories be incorporated in exams, and they might not care as much about interpretations of the theories themselves.

The same goes for every other class you will take. I even had a math professor who didn't care if we got the answer to a problem right as long as we used the correct formulas to eventually arrive at the right answer. How can this be? Because, to a mathematician, it is the *process* of the proof that is important.

The same is true, in differing ways, for nearly all courses. Why? Because in knowledge, *we can be wrong.* Just think of Copernicus, arguing with Church leaders about which celestial body revolved around the other. What is common sense now was heresy then. Here's the deeper message from your professors: if we force ourselves to think carefully and critically, we can more likely than not *find* the correct answer to a new, more interesting question tomorrow.

Each professor is different, of course, and the key is to study *your* professor. Take note of mannerisms; the way that person approaches concepts, ideas, and analysis; and how the concepts are explained.

TALK WITH YOUR PROFESSOR

You're paying a lot of money for an education, and, in addition to classroom time, your professors are available in office hours. So, visit them!

You don't want to make up stuff, of course. That would be counterproductive. (See "brown-nosing," above.) Professors pick up on this very quickly and are *very* annoyed. What you *can* do, however, is to save some of the questions you might have asked in class and ask them one-on-one instead. This way you not only get in-depth answers, but also pick up on interests, approaches, and mannerisms that are not always fully displayed in a classroom setting.

Most professors will not give valuable advice exclusively to one student. In fact, professors will inform the entire class if a student asks a particularly good question—but there's still a benefit in having been that particular student who asked that particularly good question. When you ask the next question, you're likely to get an even more in-depth answer, and you're building a rapport that might be extremely helpful when it comes time to ask for a letter of recommendation for, say, an internship.

Because professors do care about their field, they will respond positively when they see a student who is interested in learning about that field. Whether that becomes *your* field is irrelevant; you're there to learn. To the extent that you can learn with some enthusiasm...well, why not? Why waste your time learning without excitement (or not at all)?

The point is that you can learn how your professors approach issues in a more engaging setting than the classroom. Importantly, you must prepare *intelligent* questions to discuss. If you're just making stuff up, don't bother. (In other words, don't bother wasting your time going to the professor's office, and don't bother the professor with simple questions you could answer with just a quick glance through your textbook.) You also should not visit every day, or even every week. When you have a handful of *good* questions, visit and ask. Here's a hint that you're on the right track: if you're listening actively, chances are you'll have lots of good questions that aren't covered sufficiently in the textbook.

Listen. Really Listen.

Yes, this heading is repeated. Yes, each time "listen" is listed twice. That's because listening—really *listening*—is important!

Though not all professors provide practice questions, many will discuss, in general teams at least, what will be on the exams. Here's the problem: Most students want to hear, essentially, the *exact* questions the professor will use. This, of course, is not going to happen.

In truth, this provides an advantage to you…if you know how to listen. While everyone else is impatient for the exact questions, what the professor is likely to do is to alert students to the *areas* to study. Because some students don't really study—instead they end up trying to cram—what they'll miss are the subject concepts and connections the professor would like to make plain. They usually *are* plain, if you've done the reading.

So, if you have kept up and understand those major concepts, the professor's pre-exam discussions will make sense. You'll be able to focus *and* understand the exact questions when they are placed in front of you on exam day.

It's amazing how few surprises there are when you're properly prepared. This happens when you stop expecting to be told the precise questions and instead listen for the concepts the professor wishes you to know.

PRACTICE TESTS

One of the best ways to get into your professor's head is to take practice tests. This is something you'll want to do closer to exam time, of course, because you'll miss most of the issues if you attempt a practice question too early.

I had several professors who would have past exams for students who wanted to look at them, while others would give a sample set of questions, and still others who would leave us to find our own resources. If your professor does not offer practice exams, then you should ask what sources are available to test your knowledge. Your professors will be pleasantly surprised: you *want* to test yourself!

Chances are, there are "test banks" with lots of questions—but those aren't the ones your professor is likely to share. Instead, your own textbook probably has a set of questions at the end of each chapter. If not, go to the library to see if there are others that do. Check back with your professor and ask which are good questions for you to review…and would they be willing to read your responses? Chances are, your professor will be shocked (and pleased) that you are willing to actually test yourself *in their beloved field,* so they'll probably be more than willing to help you.

Taking practice tests is invaluable. Whether it's the professor's own tests or any other, you must take advantage of them. A large part of why doing so is important is not just the self-motivation—it's the fact that you will enter the test having already gone through similar tests. This means that the actual test will be almost anticlimactic; it becomes almost routine. Almost. When everyone else is approaching the exam with nervousness, not really knowing what to expect, you will enter with confidence, because you know 90 + percent of what could possibly be tested. You've *been* tested, and your professor has probably fine-tuned your thinking in your one-on-one reviews of your answers. And, of course, your professor is still deeply impressed that you care about the subject *and* are self-motivated enough to prepare as few other students do.

As to these practice questions, this means more than "…take a look at them before exams." It means blocking off time *well* before exams to take the test under timed conditions, with line-by-line dissection afterwards. This is important. You need to know not only that you're right, but also *why* you're right—and why every other answer is wrong. This might seem crazy, but it will put you so far into "A" territory that you won't ever have to worry about mere grades. Even if your college doesn't award an "A + " grade, your professor *will*…in ways even more important than a mark on a transcript. A professor is likely to respond to a superstar student with "secret" recommendations, such as research assistant positions, scholarships, internships, graduate school opportunities and contacts, and on and on.

You're not "gaming" the system or pulling one over on your professors. You should be genuinely interested in each and every subject—and even if you're not, pretend that you are, so that you'll fool yourself into being interested!

Don't try to do the minimum—or even the minimum for an "A"; try to do *more* than is necessary. You'll find that mere "excellence" as most define it is ho-hum to you. You'll also find that opportunities start opening up, as if by magic. Not only will you become more interested and more engaged, you will become more interest*ing*…and more engaging.

TALK WITH UPPERCLASSMEN

This can be hard, because you won't know anyone—at least not at first—and striking up a conversation with an upperclassman can seem daunting. It can be easy because upperclassmen are just like you...they just started last year or the year before. Most are happy to discuss the ins-and-outs of your new school, of professors and their quirks—of just about anything. Now is the time to break out of your shell. Don't be shy!

Here's the advice: try to put your anxiety aside and put yourself out there. Meet people. Every college has a zillion clubs, societies, groups, you name it.

Here's the secret: once you're actually talking to a live person, you'll find that it isn't as hard or daunting as it might have seemed, and talking to them is *very* helpful. Among other things, their advice will make you less nervous, which will be important in itself. They will give you pointers about the programs, courses, professors, exams, and how exams relate to class material. Just as important, they'll help you with the social aspects of your new experience—clubs, socializing, outings, you name it.

This is where you can actually start being picky again. Really! There are usually *so* many activities, you cannot and should not do them all. More on this later. For now, realize that if you like, say, outdoor activities, then make an effort to talk with like-minded outdoors-oriented students. There are probably kayaking clubs, hiking clubs, wilderness clubs, and on and on. That's how you can meet new people in a social setting, but with real benefits in all aspects of your college years.

It won't hurt if you don't talk with someone who has already taken a particular class, but it will almost always help if you do. I met an upperclassman during my first year, and as it turned out, he had had many of the same professors during his first year. He gave me great advice about several of them, but the most helpful information was about a pattern that one professor used on the final exam. The upperclassman showed me that this particular professor would cycle through issues on the exam and told me which issues would likely be focused on during the final. I trusted him and focused my studies in that area (while of course being prepared in other areas as well), and as it turned out, he was exactly right. I didn't study less; I studied more, but in a more focused way. That extra effort—based on his first-hand knowledge—paid off, big time. It made a huge difference for me, both when I saw the exam and when I got back the grade.

Upperclassmen have taken these same classes, from these same professors. And if the upperclassmen you're talking with were in a different course or section, chances are they know someone who did have the same professor you now have. Use their experience and insight. To do otherwise is almost willful ignorance—and what's the benefit? You should *enjoy* your college years, and chatting with fellow students should be a big part of this enjoyment. So, find things you enjoy, and mingle!

How to find these upperclassmen? The obvious answer is this: they're all around! For general courses, most everyone will have taken at least one of a handful of professors teaching that course. For courses more specific to your major, hang out at and meet people in areas that your people frequent.

Look at all those campus organizations at your school. Choose a handful that are of interest, and stop in. Strike up a conversation, and see what you like. You don't need to be out to "impress" them. (They won't be impressed.) They know what you're going through, and most are glad to point you in the right direction.

Don't go overboard. You don't need a statistically valid sampling of three-quarters of the upperclass body. You just need a handful who've taken the same professors and who might have specific advice that can (and will) be *very* helpful to you.

5

READING ASSIGNMENTS

Most courses in college have substantial reading loads, including large amounts of material that can be, well, pretty boring.

I remember taking several science classes and being really interested in the material—but being bored out of my mind when reading the actual textbook. What can I say? Many textbooks are just boring. Your professor expects you to have read the material, however, and may ask you in class to recall what you have read. They'll certainly consider it fair game for the exams. I've had many exams that asked questions not covered in class, but included in the readings.

So how do you cover all of your reading assignments in such a way that you pick up the details of what you are reading and understand how all those points fit into the big picture of the subject you are studying—all without falling into a coma? You read *effectively*. That is your next good habit.

HABIT #6: READ EFFECTIVELY

Early in college, in one session I read an entire assignment—some forty pages or so of critiques to Kant's Categorical Imperative. I finished, realizing I had *no idea* what I'd just read, much less what I was supposed to learn. I had just wasted several hours—and I *still* didn't know Kant's Categorical Imperative. Although this is more or less expected when reading Kant, it was disheartening.

Another time I spent *hours* taking extensive notes on another in-depth reading assignment. I did this so I would understand it all, perfectly, and then realized that I didn't have enough time to prepare for my other classes.

This is a dilemma. There's a continuous balancing act between doing the reading for your classes and actually understanding what it is you've read. This is particularly apparent as you get further along in your studies and the classes become more difficult. Once you get behind, it's almost *Game Over:* The farther behind you get, the harder it will be to get caught up, much less keep up.

The solution is to read effectively and to take notes only on what is most important. Below are concrete steps to get the most out of each reading assignment, to read effectively:

SURVEY EACH ASSIGNMENT BEFORE YOU READ IT

Before you even *think* about reading an assignment, look in your course syllabus and the table of contents of your textbook to find out where your assignment fits. To understand the big picture you need to know how each assignment fits together.

Your classes will follow a logical, linear path—even if sometimes it doesn't seem so. How do I know? Because that's the way each discipline is structured, and so each course is going to follow a certain path to highlight that structure. Your challenge is to figure out what that path is so that you can see and learn that bigger picture. It's easier, and it's much more interesting.

After you know where the assignment fits, read the headings and subheadings. For example, if the physics assignment you are reading is under the heading "Doppler Effect," read the heading and frame your thoughts around that subject. Before reading the section *The Doppler Effect,* briefly read over the main concepts and notes that have lead you to this point. This is the habit you will use throughout college: each principle builds on the last and provides further foundation for the next. If your notes are unclear—as they often are—go to Wikipedia or Google to read or find a summary. No, you won't ever cite to these directly; but that doesn't mean you can't use these tools for what they are—a fast, usually good introduction.

Once you have read the headings; scanned the assignment and paid attention to sub-headings, bolded or italicized phrases, etc.; and perhaps read up on the topic generally—then you're ready to dive in. I can almost hear you saying, "But this is more work!"

First, remember that your goal isn't to do the minimum. It's to be effective. This means, among other things, that you need to do more than the minimum. Second, the process I outline will make your study much more efficient, because you'll actually understand what it is you're reading, rather than have your eyes glaze over. Finally, it *won't* take more time. What is done here is done quickly. It only takes a few seconds to scan your course syllabus: a minute or so to scan the headings, phrases, etc.; and another few minutes to read about the subject online. As a result, less time is wasted when you do read the textbook or article—because it will make more sense.

Each piece is part of the puzzle that creates the "big picture." Each assignment is structured differently, but with some view towards that big picture. For example, if you're reading from a textbook, then the reading will follow a structured outline—bolded headings, sub-headings, and so on. Other assignments might be from books written in a more traditional format, be it a classic piece of literature or an essay on evolution. The format doesn't matter. What *does* matter is that you understand what's going on in the assigned reading—the part of the big picture it addresses—before you focus on its many details. You need to know where you are before you start—and one way to accomplish this is by surveying each assignment. "Survey" means what it does to a land surveyor: knowing exactly where each piece of land starts and where it ends. Surveyors are not "kind of" sure; they must *know,* and lay out precise coordinates.

Finally, most textbooks will have a list of questions or additional points at the end of each chapter or section. Scan these questions or notes as well, *before* reading the assignment. All of this is there to help you sort, understand, and remember. The assignment won't make sense if you don't understand why you're reading it; these practices will help.

CREATE YOUR OWN QUESTIONS

As you are scanning the assignment and organizing your mind for the reading, try creating a few questions about what you're reading. Write them down on a fresh sheet of paper or in a new document. Then compare those questions to the ones the book's author added to the end of that section. This will help focus your thoughts about the material and solidify your understanding.

The better your questions, the better your understanding will be. As you add questions, you'll refine them. When your mind is actively searching for answers, you are better able to understand how the concept is applied. This prepares you for questions in class and for possible exam questions.

Here's an example: if a heading says "Photoautotroph," you can make up a question such as "How is a photoautotroph different from a chloroplast?"

See how that will help with your understanding? You need to understand both to even begin to answer the question—and the exam is almost certain to touch on one if not both.

In a philosophy class you might ask "What are the differences and similarities between absurdism and nihilism?"

The questions needn't be difficult, and in fact the simpler, the better. You will begin to come up with questions in your mind without even being conscious of them. But, when you start, make the effort to be conscious about your questions before and as you read. Your mind will then automatically focus on finding the answers to the questions you've just posed.

Make up as many questions as you can, and write out a quick summary of your answers. Don't use too much time to write out each question (or answer) too extensively: simple is better, and key words are, well, key. As you read more, your answers will get better and more sophisticated.

READING

In addition to posing and answering your own questions, there is another habit that can be beneficial: read each assignment as you would a mystery novel. After all, the assignments are about *something.*

It helps in your reading if you decide—and you *can* decide this—to be excited about what you read. It's an attitude adjustment: reading because you want to learn, reading because you are excited about what comes next, reading because someone found this worth writing and you're going to be interested in finding out why.

Sure, this method might not work when an assignment is particularly dry—and in those cases you just have to push through—but most assignments involve *stories*. For example, the story of how the human genome was discovered, or how Descartes came up with a particular philosophy, or what George Washington did at a particular point in the Revolutionary War. This can be *fascinating* stuff, if you want it to be. Your assignments can be just plain interesting…if you allow yourself to be interested. If you make this small adjustment, your reading becomes more engaging and much more effective. It also won't *feel* like such a chore, and the time will pass much, much faster.

REVIEW YOUR NOTES OUT LOUD AS YOU READ

Our brains benefit from multiple sensory experiences, and when you can hear what you are writing down, you have three levels of intake to your brain. You *see* what you are reading, you *hear* what you are writing, and your writing is itself reinforcing. As you jot quick notes about your reading and answer your personal questions, you are sifting through the material and deriving the most important aspects of each. You write it down and then read it out loud. It becomes easier to remember as you go along, and what you remember you remember *better.*

A related tip is to do the same thing when reviewing drafts of your research papers. Reading a draft out loud will make most mistakes obvious, and will greatly improve your final paper—and, likely, your grade.

Once you finish your reading, scan your notes and review what you've learned. This review is not leisurely; you should review at a rapid pace. You also need to be serious—this isn't something done upside-down while fidgeting with your latest electronic toy. Work intensely, and then you can play.

If you don't remember a particular point in your notes, or if something doesn't make sense, don't move on until it is clear. If you spend several minutes and still find it unclear, then jot it down. If it still doesn't make sense after thinking about it a while, that's a question to ask your professor.

Read Only Once

This is a no-brainer. You simply cannot read assignments and then re-read them and then re-re-read them again. You simply don't have time. And even if you did, that's just a waste of time.

Yes, you might not understand what the assignment is about—although you shouldn't even be reading the assignment if you don't understand at least roughly what it's about—yet part of reading effectively is reinforcing to yourself that you will only read the assignment *once,* so you had better get everything out of it that you need to get out of it. If you stick to that rule, you will find yourself reading more carefully and ultimately getting more out of the reading assignments more quickly.

Get Rid of Distractions

We've already touched on this, but when it comes to reading it is *very* important. To read effectively you must read without distractions. You must read every word and be *actively* trying to understand and apply each sentence. This is not something you "just do": when you study, you *study!*

"Distractions" means anything that will get between you and what you're reading. If you are distracted, it will take you twice as long to read the assignment—and you won't get anything from it.

So, get rid of them!

For me, it was the internet and TV. The solution? I told myself that I would spend ten minutes online after every fifty minutes of reading, plus thirty minutes watching a television show for every three hours studying. If you do that, you'll get more done faster, leaving you more time to do whatever it was that was distracting you. Get into the habit of really paying attention to what you are reading without distractions, and you'll realize that what you are reading begins to make a lot more sense.

A related topic is going to cause a fight, I know: you cannot listen to most music you would want to listen to and still do a good job studying. No, you can't. I understand that you like music. I do too. I understand that you *think* you can listen and also concentrate—or, a favorite statement, because you're special it actually makes your studying better. Nonsense. Try a test. Listen to your favorite music at the volume you like to listen to it while reading a substantial section of a textbook. Then take a test—answer the questions at the end of that chapter. Now choose a chapter—a harder one, if you like. Do the same thing, this time without the music. Compare your results.

You cannot listen to hip hop, rock, etc., and at the same time actively comprehend. You certainly can't do it *as well.* No one can; the only difference is how badly each of us is affected by a distraction. Some a little; most a lot. A better case is made if you say you like to listen to classical or soft jazz, softly played, and if that applies to you, there's less of an objection. (But you might want to be careful around whom you display your taste.) Better is just to use your study time to...study.

So, don't try to study in a dorm (or anywhere else) when it's loud or when others are likely to come in to ask for a sheet of paper, borrow five dollars, take you along to a party, or anything else. Find a time and place where you can escape *all* of those distractions.

Focus

Only read what you have to read. You'll discover pages and pages of notes and commentary following many of your assignments. The notes can be interesting, but much of the time they aren't really necessary. This means, usually, that you shouldn't waste your time reading them. You must prioritize. You've other classes to worry about first!

Your job is to get the main point from your reading assignment and...that's about it. If there is a note or something that the professor thinks is important, chances are it will be pointed out in the syllabus or during class.

One crucial reality you should grasp early in college is that your exams can only encompass so much information. Even though they are long and cover a huge amount of material, they are still going to cover the most important stuff (or what the professor thinks is the most important within that defined body of most-important stuff).

A classmate of mine would spend hours and hours studying the most microscopic details—and wasted much of her time. The professor tested basic concepts, and the details that she thought were important simply couldn't be included in the exam. When your professors think a particular concept is sufficiently important, they will say so. Really. If you're awake in class, you'll know the major areas to be covered.

An easy way to remember this important idea is encompassed within a clichéd phrase: don't miss the forest for the trees. Get too caught up in the details—the trees—and you miss the big picture. So read the assignments carefully, but skim the notes that come afterward if you must. Just don't waste your time. Read what you need to read!

6

EFFECTIVE STUDY

One of the college tricks that will greatly increase the effectiveness of your studies is to see each course as a group of concepts that work together to create (or, more correctly, as part of) a subject. You need to see the big picture to understand how it all fits together.

THE BIG PICTURE

In an English class, for example, you might be assigned a piece of literature. You read about the author, the time period in which the work was written, the era in which the literature takes place, and other pertinent aspects to the piece. Each piece is one part of the puzzle that you will be responsible for in the course. The "puzzle" is English, or perhaps a sub-part of the field of English, such as comparative literature. So rather than trying to understand each piece of the puzzle on its own, look at how they fit together.

How does that period fit within the context of later (or earlier) works? How about the author's background? How do those factors add meaning and depth that you didn't recognize before? Are you going to read now with a different eye? If so, why? If not, why not? (After all, the professor probably wouldn't be going over the pieces if she didn't think they were meaningful.) As you do this, the big picture emerges—and changes how you see each piece of the bigger picture.

The same goes for science, math, music, philosophy, you name it. The pieces make up the whole, and once you see the whole, then each new piece is easier to understand.

THE POWER OF ASSOCIATION

Everyone learns differently. Some people construct little acronyms to remember things, while others use note cards, outlines, etc. Some people have great short-term memories—they can just shove everything into their mind a few hours before the exam and then regurgitate it on paper. For reasons we'll get into, this last method is not a good long-term strategy. One technique nearly everyone can use, however, is the power of association.

It's weird, but there are certain things that we automatically associate together. A simple example of this is with smells. We don't even have to be anywhere near a movie theater, but when we smell popcorn with butter, we think of movies. Pine trees bring to mind thoughts of Christmas, perfumes and colognes will remind us of certain people we have associated that smell with, and so on. Beyond smells, the power of association can be complex. For example, I might be in a certain place where the sights, sounds, and smells work together and bring to mind an obscure memory from childhood. There are even some movies that I automatically associate with others simply because I saw their movie trailers together.

Those who specialize in marketing tap this power of association. They flash certain images or sounds in their advertisements to make you think of something that incites good feelings and encourages you to buy their product. Think of the many times you find yourself humming a jingle from an ad as you walk through the grocery story. It's the power of association in play: as you see the product, your subconscious pulls up that song—and vice versa. If you hear a snippet of a song, or just happen to think of a jingle and start humming it, chances are much higher that you'll seek out that product.

The trick is to use this power of association in your studies. Find a way to apply this power to help you remember what you are learning. In a way, writing out the finals outline (which I'll explain later) is using association by narrowing down what you have learned to just a few words that will help your brain to recall a piece of information, which is why the outline format is so effective. More on this later.

There are other, equally effective methods that use the power of association. For example, in some college courses you might have to memorize lists of concepts. I would assign a catchy word or short phrase to a certain concept, and then memorize the words using note cards. On the exam, I could mentally flip through the list of words or phrases to find the concept that answered the question. This was easier than attempting to think through entire concepts to come to the answer—with those words and short phrases I mentally prepared a list that was easily accessible.

Others might take the same lists and, if they're musically inclined, set the concepts to music. Or, if you're mathematically talented, maybe you match them to equations. I know students who use colors to categorize the concepts they are using, and others use numbers, names, animals, etc. Anything that will be easy for you to remember and associate with a concept will make your study more effective and will help you to recall information for exams. Whatever works!

READ THE SYLLABUS

Yes, the syllabus is mundane and boring. Got it. You still need to read *every word* until you fully understand when assignments are due, what is due when, how many quizzes and exams there will be, your professor's office hours and preferred contact times, and what is expected of you, *exactly*. Read it twice if you have to, and keep it in a ready file. This is a reference, not just a scan-and-forget-it handout.

Much of the time you won't need the syllabus, as your professor is likely to talk about each assignment before it is due, and you will rarely need to contact your professor outside of the listed office hours. But an efficient student knows the syllabus just in case. It takes five minutes—maybe ten for those annoyingly long syllabi—to make sure that you aren't missing anything (assignments, formats, expectations, etc.). You must know *exactly* what you need to do for a good grade; don't give up a half-letter grade (or more) because you missed something simple.

A quick example before we move on: I had several classes where my grade could be adjusted by up to a full letter depending on my class participation, while in other classes it didn't matter if I participated during class or not—or even attended class for that matter—because the grade was based solely on exams. This is valuable information, and it is in the syllabus.

DO ALL OF YOUR ASSIGNMENTS, NO MATTER HOW SMALL

To study effectively, you should know what you are getting yourself into—at least a little bit. It would of course be impossible for me to explain how each of your courses will work and how each of your professors will grade you—but here is a simple truth: As mentioned, your grade will come primarily from your midterm and final exams. In many courses, however, you will also be given smaller assignments to complete along the way. Sometimes these are meant as crumbs tossed your way, but often they are the professor's way to prod you to study, and thus actually learn the material.

This point, while basic, is also one that needs to be emphasized: you must do *all* of your assignments. To do otherwise is just plain foolish. I know, I know—you are in college. The days of high school homework are behind you! College is different, right? Well, yes and no. You are required to study more on your own—with less direct feedback along the way—and your homework will often consist of readings to do rather than assignments to turn in. Whether it is readings or assignments, you must do it all. Do it efficiently by doing assigned readings only once and not spending too much time on each piece, but you must do each and every assignment, no matter how small.

Why? Because most professors simply will not assign points for assignments not handed in. How can they? If all you did was to hand in a piece of paper with just your name on it, you might get a mercy point. But *no* paper? Zero. Not only that, but professors are like anyone. If they see that someone is trying, they'll be more likely to give you the benefit of the doubt when they assign the final grade. If they see the opposite, they won't. Would you?

Here's another example at my expense: I had a class that was *very* difficult: Predicate Logic. The course required, several times a week, that we turn in homework assignments. The assignments consisted of a few problems and counted for only a few points. For the first half of the semester I didn't bother doing them, figuring that I would just ace the midterm and final and get the high grade that way. You can probably guess what happens when anyone *assumes* good luck. Come midterm time, I struggled to digest everything that we had gone over up to that point, and I found it very,

very difficult. When I actually took the midterm, it was a disaster. I was trying problems that I'd never even seen before. I thought that the exam was a little unfair, so I went to the professor and told him so. He pulled out his grade book and noticed that I hadn't done any of the homework assignments. Ouch. He pulled out some of the problems that he'd assigned, and to my surprise, *many of the problems on the exam were taken directly from the homework.* He also added up the points that I would have earned had I done the homework, and to my further surprise, the points would have all but evened out my atrocious midterm grade. I felt stupid. I *was* stupid for not doing those "minor" homework assignments, and it cost me. Not only did it cost me, but I also didn't actually save any time—and I suffered a *lot* more aggravation than had I simply spent a few hours each week on the problems.

I took my newly learned lesson to heart. I did every problem during the second half of that semester. I aced the final exam, and also got those few valuable points for the homework. The moral of the story is that I could have had a fantastic grade in that class, with the same or less effort and much less stress, but ended up with only a semi-good grade and lots of stress because of a very bad, very lazy habit. I made a mistake and learned a lesson that I would never forget.

Sometimes it's difficult to do each homework assignment. Okay, fair enough. But you still need to. Set aside a specific, reasonable amount of time (not too much, not too little) for each class, each day. If you follow the advice in this book, you will have more than enough time to get it all done *and* enjoy yourself at parties and social events.

Preparing for your midterm and final exams ought to be your main concern, even as you go to class and complete assignments throughout the semester. The class work and assignments will help you prepare for your exams and, as discussed above, will provide an important percentage of your final grade, directly and indirectly. As such, it is essential to keep in mind that the bulk of your grade comes from your exams. If you pass your exams, you will pass the class.

Putting the two together means this: to *ace* your class—which I assume is your real goal, as you're the type of person to read a book on how to achieve success in college—you need to do well on your exams *and* work conscientiously in all other aspects of the course. It just makes good sense: it logically follows that you need to be *extremely* well-prepared for each exam so that your whole semester (and your future career) is not flushed down the proverbial drain because of bad study habits. Everything ties together, in one way or another, in most courses. And good habits in one course are a sign that you have good habits in all courses. Be sure you are in fact well-prepared, and be sure nothing takes you by surprise.

The following habits work hand in hand with preparing for your finals, and you must do each simultaneously for this to work most effectively. Also, this might sound like a lot of work, but actually it's less work (and much less stress) than you'll face otherwise. It beats cramming a truckload of information—or, more correctly, *trying* to cram a truckload of information—for a test that has cost you an even bigger truckload of money and time.

What follows is going to be hard. It's not "hard" hard, but it *is* difficult, because it will mean that you'll need to break bad old habits and adopt better, newer ones. It also means that you will have to go against the typical collegiate routines—you must cut against the grain. Or, if you prefer a different metaphor, you will have to swim against the current.

HABIT #7: BREAK THE NOTE-TAKING HABIT. TAKE "OUTLINE" NOTES.

This is going to sound weird, especially because you've developed your note-taking skills all during high school. Worse, the feeling of necessity for taking notes in college is higher than in high school, because there's so much more to learn.

Ready? Here goes.

You have to stop taking notes. At least, you have to stop taking the stacks of notes that you're used to taking. There is simply too much for you to learn in college, and the prospect of taking extensive notes while reading *and* during class is simply absurd. Unfortunately for most students, it won't seem absurd until just before exams, as you stare at those stacks and stacks of utterly useless notes. Why useless? Because they won't help you study for your exams. Your notes are pretty much a useless stack of dead trees.

I never realized the volume of time I was wasting until I got into the time-study paradoxes in law school, where you have to study even more than in college (a whole lot more!) *and* there is even less feedback. If I'd learned this in college, I cannot even begin to tell you the quantities of time and energy I would have saved.

Allow me an illustration from law school: when I finished my first semester of property law, I had over 140 pages of notes. One hundred forty pages! In contract law, I had *one hundred eighty* pages! I had novel-length accounts for each class, and faced the overwhelming task of whittling that down to a digestible amount of material. What happened? Soon after I started to go over these notes, I realized that they were doing absolutely nothing for me. Many I could hardly recognize, and they were certainly not providing any magic clarity to any of the rules we had studied. Quite the opposite. In front of me were nearly a thousand pages of suddenly worthless gibberish.

As I wrote this book, I realized that the same lesson applied to my biology class in college, as with philosophy, film, English, and science classes. I took copious notes all through college, and it never quite clicked—until now—that I never really *used* them. And I never really used them because they were never really very useful.

Okay, I can hear it now:

"…But you *have* to know all this information!" you say.

"…But I only took notes on *exactly* what we studied in class!!" you claim.

"…It's just *crazy* to tell us *not* to take notes!!!" you protest.

Well, let's think about this from a different perspective. Imagine memorizing a novel, or even just reading it several times so you know it well. Let's make it an exciting novel (which your college notes will *not* be). Now imagine getting to know five different novels for five different exams—and imagine writing 140 pages of excruciatingly detailed analysis for each of them. It just doesn't seem possible, or if it is possible, it doesn't seem quite worth the effort.

When it comes to studying for finals, you do not want to read a novel-length account of Biology 101. The solution is straightforward and follows the theme of this book. Good study habits are also about efficiency—doing only what you have to, and doing it *very* well. To be efficient in taking notes, take only *one sheet of paper* with you to each class! Your goal is simple: *do not write any more than that single page.*

You can use the same concept when typing notes on your computer, but there you need a bit more self-control. It's harder to know when you've hit one page, and it's easier to just keep typing away. One page is all you need from each class—and in many cases, it's still too much. Even one page per day equals forty-odd pages per semester, or 200+ pages total with all of your courses combined. Too many notes!

Write down *only* what is essential for your understanding of whatever concept it is you are learning about. After all, you have already read the material (you have, right?) and taken super-condensed notes on your reading (more on that later). This habit of taking down only the most important information will not only save you time and wasted mental energy, it will also help with the process of constructing your "final study outline."

Let me describe this concept briefly: a *final study outline* is a hierarchical summary of what you've learned in that semester, including not just the many concepts and ideas you've learned but also how each concept, example, and connection fits within the structure of every other concept, example, and connection. The final study outline is how the subject you are studying is structured.

In college as well as in graduate school, outlines are a way to learn the subjects efficiently because a single sentence, or even a few words, will trigger all of the related concepts within that part of the outline. An efficient student will create an outline, read it a few times (and refer to it while working through practice exams)—and then cut the outline in half. That's right! You're going to chop your outline down to size—a manageable size that will actually help you, instead of adding to the fog of confusion before finals. This process of condensing your outline will be repeated until there are only a few words or lines for each concept. This is sometimes called the *summary outline*. Even then, there's still quite a lot of information to learn. This is why outlines are so important.

One analogy, when it comes to studying for college, applies: studying for your exams is like a rocket being launched into space. When the rocket uses up the fuel in its primary and secondary boosters, they are detached from the rocket. Likewise, when you study for your finals, you first read your textbook and go to class. Once these are done, they are *done*—and those parts of your learning process detach and fall away. You read a chapter of your textbook and put what you need into an outline. That chapter then falls away. You then edit your outline, and every piece deleted is a bit of unusable junk. All this happens until you have created your super-efficient final outline. You don't need the other stuff—you don't *want* all that other stuff—because you *know* it. At this point, your super-efficient outline is to help remind you of everything that you already know.

So if you're going to whittle down your notes into an outline anyway, why not take "notes" that will go directly into your outline? This means that you read your assignments effectively—so you know what is going on in class—and you actively participate in class. You put your efforts into selective notes, which go immediately into your outline—which you then progressively edit to produce a super-efficient outline.

For the record, I never did read all those hundreds of pages of notes. They went right into the trash. I still did very well on my exams, despite all that waste of valuable time and energy. I can't even imagine how much better I would have done (or how much more time I would have enjoyed) had I not wasted so much time.

HABIT #8: WRITE YOUR OWN OUTLINES

Writing outlines isn't particularly hard. But it is time consuming. It can also seem overwhelming, especially if you wait until the last minute to start. And for some courses, commercial outlines or some form of Cliff Notes-like products or online goodies lurk in the shadows, tempting you to throw down your own notes and read a pre-packaged outline in place of writing your own. As tempting as these are, these are no substitute for your own work, both in creating and in refining your outline; without that effort, you simply won't get enough out of it. It's not about the outline itself; it's about your brain.

So how do you write an outline? The first and most accurate step is to write down the major chapter headings first. You will find these headings in your book, and also, quite likely, in your syllabus. If there's a difference between them, follow the syllabus. You will include specific points—initially and during the semesters—to tie the "official" facts to your professors' individual takes on each subject.

STANDARD OUTLINE

For example, in a highly simplistic and non-exhaustive outline for biology, starting with the concept of *photosynthesis,* you might start with these headings:

1. Photosynthesis

2. Equation

3. Photoautotroph

4. Chloroplasts

Once you have written down the headings, add the definitions and details as you read and attend class, like so:

1. Photosynthesis

2. Equation: $2n\ CO_2 + 2n\ H_2O +$ photons
   $2(CH_2O)n + n\ O_2 + 2n\ A$

   a. Carbon dioxide + electron donor + light energy
      carbohydrate + oxygen + oxidized electron donor

3. Photoautotroph: an organism that can synthesize food directly from carbon dioxide using energy from light

4. Chloroplasts: organelles found in plant cells and other eukaryotic organisms that conduct photosynthesis. Chloroplasts capture light energy to conserve free energy in the form of ATP and reduce NADP to NADPH.

   a. Chloroplast ultrastructure:
1. outer membrane
2. intermembrane space
3. inner membrane (1 + 2 + 3: envelope)
4. stroma (aqueous fluid)
5. thylakoid lumen (inside of thylakoid)
6. thylakoid membrane
7. granum (stack of thylakoids)
8. thylakoid (lamella)
9. starch
10. ribosome
11. plastidial DNA
12. plastoglobule (drop of lipids)

   b. Cellular structure

   c. Cell membrane

   d. Cell wall

   e. Nuclear membrane

   f. Plasmodesma

And so on...

It looks like a lot—especially if you've not had biology in a while. But, once you're in class, preparing for each class and getting organized around each topic, it's really quite logical. As you proceed, your study gets more in-depth and your outline fills up, become more detailed.

More important, how are you going to remember that formula? Well, you're going to remember it because you're going to use it! You're going to repeat it, in writing and by hearing it (because you're reading it out loud), and you're going to go over the explanation about how the components of carbon and water and photons and carbohydrates and oxygen interrelate. It really *is* fascinating (if you let it be), and before you know it, *it all makes sense!*

The logical stopping place is the point at which the outline is too cryptic to make sense. But don't worry about this to start, because you will begin to understand the subject *intuitively.* That's when you know you're on your way to mastering that subject.

Then something else magical happens: you won't need all those words! Why? Because you'll already understand why biologists have organized everything the way they have. So you condense your outline, removing words and explanations—because you *know* the explanations and don't have to re-read them. It's similar to why we don't have to repeat "A," "B," "C," and so on, in sequence when writing out a word—we of course already know our ABCs, and so we simply...*write out the word.* That's the level of understanding you're looking for in class.

Here's a sample of a first-round condensed section, after you've studied for a while:

1. Photosynthesis

    a. Equation: $2n\ CO_2 + 2n\ H_2O$ + photons $2(CH_2O)n + n\ O_2 + 2n\ A$

    b. Photoautotroph: organism that can synthesize food from CO_2 using photons.

    c. Chloroplasts: organelles in cells and other eukaryotic organisms that capture light energy to conserve free energy as ATP and reduce NADP to NADPH.

You would complete each section as you prepare for the class in which that topic will be discussed. It's crucial that you prepare *before* you actually go to class. Don't rely on the class to tell you what's important: you should go into class *knowing* what is important!

After class, you will continue the process of refining and editing your outline down to a super-condensed and highly usable version. At that point, your outline will once again resemble the chapter headings with the main words and points to remind you of what you've learned. This becomes both a symbol of what you know—and *the* best way to study for finals.

BULLETED OUTLINE

The above photosynthesis example is a simple outline, and it works to prepare for most exam types you will face. You can benefit from different styles of outlines for different classes, however.

A bulleted outline worked well for me in courses in literature, for example, where I was to know certain facts about authors and their works. The bulleted outline was beneficial in this context because themes in a literary piece could be listed and easily organized and cross referenced with other works of literature—all in preparation for the exam. The bulleted outline also works for courses where you have to recall certain facts that go under a common category—like a date. In a history class, for instance, you would list a certain place and time and list the pertinent facts. Below is another example of how this type of outline would look. (It would be more detailed when you get finished with it, of course.)

George Orwell

- Born June 25, 1903, as Eric Blair

- Popular journalist, essayist, and novelist

- Best known for his efforts in journalism and reportage of English culture, as well as his novels *Nineteen Eighty-Four* and *Animal Farm*

- Won the Prometheus Award in 1984 for his contribution to dystopian literature

Albert Camus

- Born November 7, 1913

- French Algerian author, philosopher, and journalist

- Gave rise to the philosophy of absurdism; actively opposed nihilism

- Contemporary of George Orwell

- Camus' novel The Plague is similar in style and theme to Orwell's *Nineteen Eighty-Four*

Another possibility is a chart that outlines related or conditional ideas. Conditional ideas are iterative, or in other words will change depending upon the prior condition. In programming and other fields, this is the "decision tree," or a series of decisions that branch out like the limbs of a tree. A chart of this type would look like this.

As you can see, there's almost limitless room for additional conditions: "Are the sprinklers turned on but the main is turned off…?" Believe it or not, if and when you take philosophy, you'll be surprised at the level of detail you'll cover (and be expected to know) with a simple statement *The street is wet.* Not only will you delve into logic, but you'll also discuss the implications that go along with the many heretofore hidden aspects of a wet street.

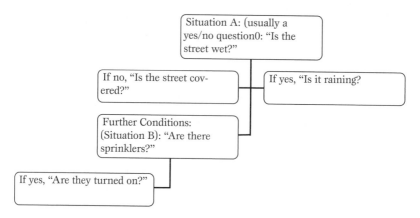

I didn't use this method for entire courses—but you certainly could, if you had a big enough piece of paper. (There are, of course, commercial charts for this—but again, it's important not to rely solely on those.) With new software, making charts and maps is relatively simple and works well for those who like to learn more visually. For Windows users, take a look at a program called *Visio,* and for Mac users, try *Omnigraffle.* Both programs will help you easily create charts that you can use to better understand your notes. Following is an example of how a chart might be used as a visual outline.

There are many ways to do these, of course. The key is not merely to copy, but to put it in a form that is both accurate and makes sense to you. Once you start to do this, you'll be amazed at just how helpful these will be—not least in producing presentations that astonish your classmates and professors (and, later, bosses) when you have to give them. You benefit in multiple ways, and you will "suddenly" be valuable among your classmates for your skills.

Charts and maps don't work for every type of outline just as bulleted outlines or traditional outlines don't work every time either. For many of your courses, you could have an expansive chart that goes on for page after page and branches off to different topics, so much that at some point you lose the advantage of compiling an outline. The same goes for the bulleted outline, which is good for things like rules and facts (which tend to have same-level data), but not as good for concepts that contain detailed elements (which tend to be more hierarchical and thus need different outline levels to show the interrelationships).

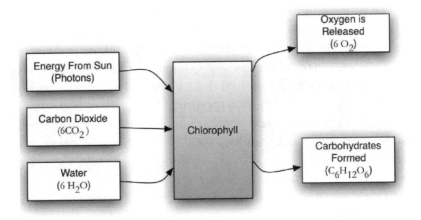

Remember: your outline is a *tool* to study more effectively. Yet it can become something that *hinders* your study and exam preparation if you aren't careful. You have to know the material you're putting into an outline and choose what kind of outline suits the material best. Many times, like the example above, you will use one type of outline—like the chart—for a small part of the information while the rest of the information is contained in a more traditional, hierarchical form. It's your outline. Experiment!

Outlining is a process. As you learn this information you will, after a while, not need all of it. So, the closer you get to your finals, the *smaller* your outline should get. By exam time you should have a handful of super-condensed outlines, one for each course, with the details all but memorized because you've *used* them repeatedly. This is a form of memorization, but better: The resulting outlines are not only easier to study, but the process of getting to super-condensed outlines helps you learn the material inside and out.

If you want to learn in the best way possible, write your own outlines. You will know and understand the concepts better if you write your own, and you will *not* know and understand the concepts as well if you "borrow" someone else's or use only a commercial one. Can you use those? Sure. But they're not the end result—that is what happens in your mind. Everything else is a tool. Outlines force you to understand what you're writing, especially when you get to the condensing part of outlining.

Okay. That written: use supplementary materials.

Reading commercial study outlines (available in most places where textbooks are sold) is also a useful way to prepare for class. You will get an idea of where the class is going, and the professor's lectures will make more sense. Commercial study guides are resources I never really noticed until I was in law school, mainly because they are probably more pertinent to success in law school. Cliff Notes are the nearest popular comparison in college. These guides are available and can help you in navigating whichever subject you're studying. They won't be available for every class, but you could certainly ask your professor if he or she has any ideas of good guides. (They almost certainly will not recommend Cliff Notes, which are seen as just above cheating.) Most of the time, your professor will point you in the right direction to other materials. And aside from commercial guides, there is a growing collection of online guides—just be careful, as the quality can be uneven.

Here's what's really important: study guides are not to be used *in place of* doing your own work. They can help you know what's coming next, they will help you prepare for class, and they can help you structure your own outlines in a logical flow of information. When preparing for class, if your professor covered topics A and B last week, it is likely that you will go over topic C and possibly topic D this week. So prepare for topic C at the very least. What's the worst that can happen? You prepare for C and your professor pulls out topic E. Big deal. You wouldn't have been prepared for topic E anyway, and this way you'll already have topic C under your belt—

and you'll probably understand topic E better because you've nailed topics A, B, *and* C.

Sure, use and learn from the commercial study guides and other materials, and rely on them without feeling guilty—because they're both effective and efficient!—but don't use them *instead of* learning the material yourself. Supplements should be, well, supplemental. A good habit is using these supplements to *supplement* your work, to help it make more sense. A bad habit is simply using supplements to avoid doing the real work yourself. Professors will know the difference, and your grades will suffer.

HABIT #9: ADD TO YOUR OUTLINES DAILY

Two of the most effective study habits a student can develop are to outline *each day* before class, and to incorporate the few class notes *each day* into your outline. This takes less time overall—just a few minutes at a time—and if you do this the task of writing outlines is not so overwhelming. In fact, it's quite manageable: you are just adding a few notes to your outline each day. Before long, you will have something that is quick, easy, and worth studying.

OUTLINING FOR OPEN-BOOK EXAMS

Your outlines should be pretty much the same for both open-book and closed-book exams, and you should be equally prepared for both. Do not fall into the trap of relying on materials you can take into the exam. These are not a security blanket; they are a trap. If you *do* rely on these, you will most likely not study as hard as you need to and will end up wasting your precious exam time searching for answers. Ideally, you should know the material so well that you shouldn't even have to *look* at your outline.

One benefit to an open-book exam is that you can bring in your super-condensed outlines, each containing the concepts for just one topic. I wrote the concepts out in short statements so that, however I answered each question, I immediately knew what elements I needed to discuss. A super-condensed outline is a cue for answers you already know—thus it's easy to ace an exam.

If you have a list like this and you understand and can write out every single element, then you have accomplished your goal of being efficient *and* effective. When you reach this point, you are ready to take your exam, whether it is open book or not. This is the end goal, to be able to see a word like "photosynthesis" and just *know* everything you need to know. *That's* when you're ready!

Another way to prepare for an open-book exam is in knowing where in your outline you have each concept. I did this by putting tabs into my outline and compiling a short table of contents. That way, if I did have to open my outline, then I would know with minimal effort exactly where to find the section I needed.

Again, although it is fine to take your outline into an open-book exam, you should not *rely* on being able to look up information. Rather than some unknowable, anxiety-filled "examination" with elements you could swear you've never seen before, the test should be almost a review of basics.

If you develop these good habits and truly prepare for each final, you won't worry about the "open versus closed" conundrum, and you won't need to take your outline into the test with you. You will in fact be at an advantage either way.

HABIT #10: PLAN ONE DAY PER WEEK TO REVIEW FOR EACH FINAL

I remember a feeling of panic when I started college. I didn't really know where to even *start.* The experience was overwhelming until I got some advice from an upperclassman who suggested something simple: set aside *one day a week to review for the final.*

The best way to do this is to set aside one day a week to review your outlines for a particular class. Just reading over your outlines once a week will better prepare you for your course *and* for the final exam. Throw in practice exams and you're going to be very well prepared.

Think about it this way: what do most students do? Take lots of notes, and then read and re-read those notes, over and over again. It shouldn't take too much imagination to agree that reading your notes over and over again will be mind-numbingly boring— so boring that you will seek something less awful to do. Outlines are not boring, because they're *your* work, and they contain ideas for the entire subject in easily digestible chunks, set out in the way you (and the professor) see it.

Sure, sometimes you've got to shake it up a bit and try something new—something that will help you review your outlines but doesn't add to any boredom factor. I made flash cards out of my outlines and sometimes recorded my outlines into a podcast and listened to my notes. I know someone who drew a simple comic book that illustrated what he was learning! Perhaps if you're musically inclined, you can write a song. There are many ways to review, and it boils down to what you're willing to do and what works best for you. Yet the idea remains simple: reserve time to do an overall review of each subject at least once a week, working consistently toward your end goal...success on the exam.

You'll add more exam-preparation time and less outline-review time to this schedule once you get closer to exams. Or, more correctly, outline-review time becomes exam-preparation time. The two fit together. A review of each subject once a week will keep things fresh in your mind and help you understand each part of the course at a deeper level. Both will help you work toward your end goal of a high grade—perhaps the top grade—on the final exam.

DETAILS

College is a unique environment. In addition to the many social elements of college life, the assumptions behind your professors' actions are about a whole different world, the life of the mind. This refers to the idea that academics are interested in *ideas*. These ideas are what the university is all about. So while most students are worrying about exams and jobs (or just having a good time), most professors are thinking about ideas, because that's what *they* like. We can delve into a subject to learn what we want to learn—and if you're *enjoying* that (as a professor usually does), chances are you're doing a great job.

Efficient and effective study should not be confused with shutting out those extra details that, with the right mindset, are interesting. And we *should* try to be interested, if only because that makes the time pass by much faster and better, and we learn more and better and easier.

So, be sure you spend enough time studying the materials you will be *graded* on, and *then* delve into extra details to your heart's delight. These details, by the way, are the source of good questions to ask professors, because they underscore that you're actually interested enough in the subject to even be aware of these details. Who knows? You might find a way to add some of those details into the exam for an extra point or two—but the bulk of the points will come from getting the basics right.

You'll find that the more effective your study is, the more time you will have to focus on whatever else you want. That's how you can make this interesting *and* not have to worry about pesky things like mere grades.

Another key to effective study is staying organized, which is the next habit we will discuss:

HABIT #11: BECOME AND STAY ORGANIZED

This seems such a simple habit. All you have to do is to stay organized, right? In reality, only a few people can do this without serious effort; most others cannot.

I am not one of those who can easily stay organized, especially with stacks of printed pages, books, assignments from multiple classes, handouts, and all those crazy things we just accumulate in our bags and lockers and desks. If you let this get out of hand, the result is a mountain of junk that takes up too much space, time, and mental energy—and is demoralizing.

I am familiar with those awful moments when you realize you need just those few sentences jotted down on that random piece of paper—somewhere in that mountain of junk! You then sift through *hundreds* of pages to find it (*if* you ever find it). That is being neither efficient nor effective.

The same concept carries over to your computer. If you don't use logical names for your folders and documents and then save documents in their proper folders with a logical hierarchy, you can (and will) waste enormous amounts of time trying to locate tiny bits of needed information. Worse, you *know* that it's there, somewhere, and you know that every second is completely wasted: with a better system you would have had the answer already. Developing a good habit is a way to combat this issue, though for many—like me—it certainly doesn't come naturally.

I decided that my life as a student needed better organization. I was up to my ears in disorganization and decided to get organized, cold turkey. I was surprised to find that it did not take a lot of time to set everything in its place, and it felt uplifting! It was *well* worth it. The real challenge was in staying organized.

Your goal should be to start out organized, with a clear idea of where you put certain things—both on your computer and in your personal space. If you are like me and things easily fall into disarray, these principles still apply, but it will take a bit longer to get to that good starting point. Either way, it is worth the effort. Staying organized helps you to be more efficient: if you don't have to look for every tiny thing you need, the extra time you "suddenly" have will make your study that much more effective.

For your home, I suggest getting filing boxes or a filing cabinet. Get a bunch of folders and label them as specifically as possible. I used certain colors for different courses and then had folders for handouts, returned assignments, notes from class, notes from reading, outlines, practice exams, and miscellany. I also had a separate drawer for all of my papers and files not related to school, so as not to get them mixed together. (The same frustration and stress ensues when looking for a simple insurance form in the mix of a thousand pages of random class notes. Ugh!)

On your computer, you need to do the same things. You have to keep documents labeled as specifically and uniformly as possible, with clearly and logically arranged folders. You should think about and follow a clear and easy naming system for new versions of your work. At first, for example, I would just label the document something like: assignment (I), assignment (II), assignment (III), and so on for each consecutive draft. Unfortunately, on the day I was supposed to turn in the paper, I was in a hurry and forgot how many drafts I had. I didn't think to check before sending the assignment. I ended up sending the wrong draft, and I missed valuable points on the assignment with mistakes I had already corrected. *Arghh!* This lesson stuck with me, because it was 100% my fault: it would never have occurred had I used a better naming system.

My recommendation is to have a folder for drafts and a separate folder for the current document you are working on. The folder for the current work should only have one document in it while all others are moved to the drafts folder once they become older drafts. It takes a little more effort, but a little extra effort here and there helps you be more organized.

If you don't like that idea, then make sure you save drafts in *only* the same folder, and date each to indicate when you worked on it last. Re-save a file whenever you're making revisions so that it will be immediately clear which is the latest version. In fact, get into the habit of saving your files often. And if there's even the slightest need for a different version, save it with a new, logical name, such as

BIO 101, Assignment 4, edit 2.1 with table, 02-01-20xx

Finally, before sending an assignment, check to make *absolutely* sure that it's the right one. Open the file. Double- and triple-check your last changes, to confirm that they're where you expect them to be. Just a few minutes here can save a *lot* of headache. Getting into this habit will even save you headaches and strife in your future career as well.

Also, before you submit it, rename it again. Use a name that *your professor* will find easy to use (if the syllabus doesn't specify a format). Keep in mind that your professor might have to keep track of dozens of documents, for each assignment, multiplied by several courses! They have better things to do than to try to keep track of which document belongs to which student.

Here's an example:

Student Smith, BIO 101, Assignment 4, due 02-10-20xx.

This is a skill learned by successful people, by the way: thinking not just about themselves, but also about how they can best interact with (and help) others. Get out of your own mind! Make it easier for the *other* person, not just yourself.

Whatever your methods, you should be constantly striving to stay as organized as possible. Remember, the whole point of this is to be more effective and efficient. Being organized is a key factor to both. No matter where you are in school or how organized you are (or think you are), there's always room for improvement. Implement good organization as a consistent habit, and not only will your other good habits play out better and more easily, but you will also find yourself enjoying your college experience more, with less worry.

7

EXAMS

This is where your efforts pay off. Although developing the habits of efficient and effective study will ultimately improve your skills in your future endeavors, right now you are focused on and concerned about these habits to further one goal: *acing* your exams.

This book is a guide to establish basic good habits at the onset of college. Once you develop these habits, you will do well and you will be prepared, but even so you still have obstacles to face in the middle and at the end of your courses…midterm and final exams. College exams will be harder than other exams you have taken before. You will face multiple-choice exams that might have trickier components; essay questions that call for extended, thoughtful, in-depth responses; and short-answer questions that require specific, detailed answers with little room for fluff.

This might not sound perilous, but when you remember that all or nearly all of your grade rests on those few exam questions, the pressure starts to build. And with every piece of additional information during the year—information that is necessary for the exam—the pressure can get agonizing.

I cannot tell you that the exams aren't hard. They are. But I can tell you that if you are prepared, the experience can actually be pleasant. Instead of, say, a three-hour session racking your brain or trying to organize your thoughts, you get to show off! It takes work to get to that point, but it is achievable. You really can be an efficient and effective student—anyone can do it, and anyone can do it well. But "doing it" isn't just *talking* about doing it, or *thinking* about doing it, but *actually* doing it. Besides the habits necessary to prepare for the exam, it might be a good idea to review an exam-taking routine.

ROUTINE EXAM TAKING

When you sit down to take your first college exam, you should obviously be prepared with the material you are expected to know.

You should also be well-prepared for an extended period of time when you have to think hard and answer questions quickly, all the while sitting still among other students who are equally hard at work. This means that you should have practiced at least one exam for each class. One *full* exam. Some professors might provide past exams on which you can practice—and we've already discussed this as a method of studying *and* preparing. However, these tests can also be beneficial for test-taking practice in itself and developing your own personal strategies. Below are a few pointers to make your practice exam sessions more beneficial.

First, do the things you would do before a regular exam. With your practice exams, you want to create the exam-taking atmosphere as best as you can, so you have a better idea of what it is like.

Second, time yourself. Part of the stress and strain of a college exam is the demand to recall a large amount of information within a set time. Part of this exercise is being strict about your time. This means that you turn off your cell phone and all distractions for the amount of time you are practicing and you focus on the exam. You will be surprised at how fast the time goes when you are concentrating intensely, so it is good to get an idea of how to gauge your progress.

Third, take your practice exams around the same time you will take your real exams. If your exams are going to be in the morning, then it is a good idea to wake up and start your exam whenever your other exams will start, so you get your brain and body used to the idea of sitting and thinking during that time of the day. You probably heard this advice when studying for the SAT or ACT, and it applies here as well. You need your brain to be used to the rigors of exam taking at the time of day when you will take your exams. Otherwise, your brain might not kick into gear until midway through (or even later), which would of course raise some difficulties in the real exam.

Fourth, get sample answers from your professors and grade yourself as hard as you can. Then, try to do better. Also, when you have done a serious job reviewing your own work—which should take at least as long as the exam did—see if there are question marks remaining. If so, and if you cannot adequately address them yourself, consider asking the professor during office hours.

Finally, don't take too many practice exams like this, or you'll end up burning out. If you take these practice exams just like you would a real exam, the experience is intense. Take just enough that you are used to sitting down and actually taking (and acing) the exam. No one can tell you when enough is enough—just remember that you've still got to run the marathon. What I did, after taking a few of these practice tests, was to practice by outlining the answer to the questions rather than write them completely—but that's only after you've done full exams yourself. There is no shortcut. What there *is*, however, is an efficient, effective path.

YOUR EXAM RITUAL (LEADING UP TO THE ACTUAL EXAM)

You are prepared! So, you won't have to cram for the exam the night before. Part of your exam ritual should be going to bed at a decent time the night before. I know I've made a reference to this several times, but if you think about your exams the same way you would think about running a marathon, then you *will* be prepared. Part of the grueling experience of running a marathon is getting enough sleep before running the race. Likewise, you should get enough sleep before an exam. You need your body refreshed and your brain alert.

Your ritual can include anything that helps you get your mind going and ready for the exam. I get nervous before tests, so much of my ritual is trying to relax. I stop studying at about 6:00 p.m. the night before the exam and then focus on having an enjoyable evening. I eat a nice dinner—nothing too heavy—and then relax with my wife and kids before going to bed early.

I usually do some yoga after waking up and focus during the pre-exam morning on breathing normally and centering my mind. I have a small breakfast of eggs and toast and listen to Mozart on the way to school. Brain music! About an hour before the exam, I look over my outline, but do nothing too in-depth. If I don't know it by this time, I certainly won't learn it well enough for the exam. I don't try to "learn" anything at the last minute; I just try to prepare mentally. You will be in a similar boat, having spent a great deal of time studying and reading and preparing—all of it has passed through your mind and can be recalled.

I want to point out two aspects of my routine that might be worth further discussion. The first is a small breakfast of eggs. I read somewhere that eggs have selenium, which is a chemical that affects the brain in positive ways. The article also pointed out that even the smell of cooking eggs is beneficial to getting the brain working fast and that it helps keep your memory sharp. Regardless of the actual effects, I have eaten eggs with the belief that it helps me to think better because they contain a mind-enhancing chemical. Maybe eating eggs really does help and maybe it doesn't— maybe all I've done is to give myself some version of a placebo and I only believe that it is helping me think more clearly. Whatever eggs do, I am convinced that I perform better when I eat a nice egg breakfast.

Likewise, I've read studies that say if you listen to Mozart, you are able to recall information more easily. I've read other studies that say this just isn't so, and if it is, then the improvement is minimal. Whatever the actual effect, I've convinced myself that I can remember things faster and more clearly when I listen to Mozart prior to taking exams. It is an added assurance that I am doing everything in my power to do well—including a hearty breakfast and stimulating my mind to get both body and mind ready for the exam.

I strongly believe that you should use these positive assurances in putting your brain in proper working order. It is the whole idea behind the pre-exam ritual. You do things because they make you feel better, decrease anxiety, and help you think more clearly. The whole point of the semester prior to the final exam is to prepare for the final exam, and I view the moments just before the exam as a time to clear the mind and focus my thoughts and energies on doing well. However you focus on doing well is up to you, but it is important to do something.

How Professors Write Exams

Professors write exams to contain all of the major topics in that subject—after all, they've spent a few months teaching you this stuff and want you to show what you've learned. Exams are set up to test your knowledge of the course and are constructed to capture the forest rather than the trees, mostly. Do you remember the section on trying to see the whole picture and not getting caught up in the details? As before, that concept pertains not only to effective study but also to your exams. Each exam will have many, many trees—or facts, or specific points of the course—but the focus is how those details work together as a whole—the forest. Therefore, you should focus on the big issues and work your way to the smaller issues (and smaller and smaller issues, as you master each level). It is the bigger picture that will get you more points on the exam.

Consider this example, using the forest and the trees analogy. Let's say that a professor sits you down with a large picture of rolling hills blanketed with trees. For purely aesthetic purposes, let's say that it is autumn and the leaves are brilliantly colored. The professor asks you to describe the forest and tells you that you will be graded based on your description. So you go about analyzing the shadows from one clump of trees and how the shadow affects another group of trees. You look at dips in the rolling hills, and high points, how the sun is reflected. Several of the individual trees are prominent, and you briefly pay attention to those, but your main focus is on the forest as a whole and how all the trees work together to create the picturesque scene before you. The professor returns and you find that you missed a few things, but for the most part you did what was asked. The professor asked you to describe the forest, not particular branches or leaves or twigs or silkworms. Had you focused your attention on each individual branch or leaf, you could never have seen how the trees work together, because there is simply not enough time to get every leaf and every branch into your description without leaving out another, equally important leaf or branch. Keep in mind that the professor likes the forest. Sure, he also knows the trees—but it's the forest that is the meaning of his life's work.

This is how college classes work, as well as the final exams. Your professor can't possibly hit every detail, because there are too many details and caveats in whatever subject you are studying (it doesn't matter which), and if you highlight one, then others are just as important and probably should be mentioned. It's a slippery slope of too much information. Yes, if the professor has talked about specific trees, you had better know those. The prominent details will be there—but for the most part you should be concerned about how all the concepts you've studied work together to create the big picture of "physical science" or "English 101."

So, while the details are interesting and good to know, they should not be the *focus* of your studies or in your answers. Not only will you miss the big picture, but you could also end up spending all of your time on the details of one question and not nearly enough time on the main points of any other question. It's also likely that you'll miss a big issue entirely, resulting in many lost points.

CRAMMING

No.

If you are prepared, you will not have to cram. You will not *want* to cram. If you *have* to cram...you're already in trouble.

If you find yourself in need of cramming, however, here are a few pointers: start cramming as early in the day as possible. Yes, for many the idea of cramming is to go late into the night, pushing absolutely as much information into your brain as possible. However, remember that you will have to write comprehensible and coherent sentences the next day; being tired does not work. So start cramming as early as possible, so you can go to bed early enough to get a good night's sleep. In many ways, the sleep might be more important to your exam performance than the cramming.

Avoid caffeine and other stimulants. Instead, eat energizing foods that provide the same amount of stimuli—just in a form that your body will better use. If you don't already have an idea of these types of foods, research this before you're in college, such as by typing "healthy food for energy" in Google. If your body is already used to stimulants like caffeine, then it probably isn't a good idea to stop caffeine intake immediately before an exam. Remember, avoid sudden lifestyle changes in college—and especially before an exam. The idea is not to put anything into your body that it isn't used to. That said, I will re-emphasize that you want to be healthy and not consume stimulants that make you *feel* more energized for short periods of time but then send you crashing later.

Cram for only short periods of time, taking short breaks. Don't overdo it only to burn out. If you have to, set an alarm so you only study for 20-30 minutes at a time, max, and then take a five-minute break. When you are studying, you need to *really* study. It should be intense, which is how to maximize its effectiveness.

Don't rewrite your notes, and don't spend time formatting outlines or even re-digesting all of your notes. If you've followed the steps in this book, you will find your study sessions more focused, as you will have already prepared outlines and have already spent time going over this material. There won't be "cramming" because there won't be a need to cram. If worse comes to worse, read over your class notes and finals outline *once*—to derive quickly as much of the professor's nuances as you can—and then try to condense your notes as much as possible, using the power of association discussed above. Again, *you do not want to cram!*

Be *prepared* for your exams instead.

YET MORE TIPS

Realize that the mental strain is half the challenge. The exams are meant to put you on the spot and make you think hard. Breathing helps in reducing strain and in getting oxygen to your brain. Thus, focus on maintaining control over your breathing throughout the exam. Focus on breathing as you read and write. Practice this.

When you get the exam, stop. Read the exam instructions—every line—so as to not miss anything the professor expects. Read the entire exam first so you know what you are getting yourself into, and also so that you can divide your time appropriately. This relates to the earlier section on how professors divide the questions and grade the exams. One time I answered a second question embedded within a first question without realizing it, because I hadn't read beyond the first question. I ended up wasting a *lot* of time.

FOR MULTIPLE CHOICE EXAMS:

Again, read every line of every question and every possible answer. It doesn't matter if you find the right answer in the options—there might be a better answer down the line.

If there is no penalty for wrong answers (as there usually is not), you'll of course want to answer every question. Cross out the obviously wrong answers, and make an educated guess. Stick with your gut—as it usually is right.

FOR ESSAY AND SHORT-ANSWER EXAMS:

Outline your question before writing down any of the answer. Write down all of the major course concepts, and then work yourself through the elements of each concept.

Look at each element from every angle. The highest grades will usually go to those students who understand not only the major concepts, but also how those concepts fit together *and* how variations on those concepts apply. Explore all possible angles and perspectives.

Be fast, but be organized. Use clear, short sentences.

Allocate a certain amount of time to each question or section, and stick to that. Don't give a question more time than it will give you back in points.

For *every* issue, state the issue, your rationale, your analysis, and your conclusion. Most professors don't care what your conclusion is (unless it's way off base or differs greatly from their clearly expressed views in class); they want to see you work through the issue and analyze all the possibilities. So, everything before the conclusion is as important as the actual conclusion.

You don't need to use clever transitions from one part of a question to another. Use subheadings instead. (See "Be fast, but be organized," above.) Clear, short, simple, fast.

Don't repeat yourself.

Don't repeat the facts—start with the actual issues. You are showing the professor that you have learned what he or she has taught and can analyze the issues based on the facts.

Don't repeat yourself.

Once you are finished, relax and spend a few hours decompressing. Then get cracking on your next exam. Remember, work now and play later. Once all of your exams are done, *then* you will be in good shape to go out and have some good ol' fashioned college fun.

8

BEFORE YOU START

Your palms will be sweaty before you actually start college. Your heart will start to flutter as you realize that the moment when you leave your home and encounter the world on your own has finally arrived. With that nervousness comes a certain joy at the prospect of starting school. Maybe it's because of all the movies and television shows we've seen, but the idea of college is certainly a romantic one. Depending upon which part of the country you're in, the colors on the trees will be readying the advent of autumn; the warm summer weather will be slowly fading; parent and students will be milling about, with parents going through their own thoughts as they remember their children with braces seemingly the prior week and in diapers a week before that; and you'll be anxious and excited and every emotion in between.

I remember being in your shoes only a couple of years ago. I can still taste the uncertain nervous excitement of the experience. I remember feeling anxious about my classes, about what I was going to do with the rest of my life, much less what major I would choose. I could tell you to brush those anxieties aside, but it would do no good—you are *going* to be nervous and uncertain. You *should* be nervous—at least a little. I might even tell you that college isn't really all that hard, but that would not be telling you the truth. There will be classes that are hard, and some that will be very *very* difficult. I still have nightmares of an economics course that absolutely threw me for a loop. (In my defense, the final exam did have nine possible answers for each question, and they all seemed to be trick questions.)

What I will tell you is that you can do it, and you can be successful. In order to be successful, however, you need to establish some positive habits from the beginning—aside from those we've already discussed. (If you find yourself already deep in the collegiate experience as you read this, just remember it is never too late to develop these good habits, and refocusing your efforts in a positive way will be worth it.)

The following habits are foundational, and work hand in hand with the habits that help you in your efforts toward success. The next of these good habits—and one of the most important of all in life as well as in school—is to make a plan and stick to it.

Habit #12: Make a Plan and Stick To It

I hit two extremes in my first three weeks of college. When I first arrived, I was meeting up with friends I hadn't seen in awhile. There were several "orientation" parties not affiliated with the school and several "kick-off" parties that were.

To make matters worse, I was an avid skier and had been living away from the slopes for several years, and—like a welcome home present—it snowed early in the mountains that year, causing the ski resorts to open. Needless to say, although I was attending class, my focus on school pretty much stopped as soon as I left the classroom. The first week went by in a blur, and I missed out on the time that most students spent getting into the groove of things. I didn't pay attention those first classes of each semester where the professors go over the focus and scope of their classes and give insight into expectations—and thus how to succeed in class. I missed getting to know others in my classes who would eventually be valuable study partners. In a very real sense, I wasted my first week.

I came to this realization, hard, on the Monday following the first day of class, when a professor gave us a quiz on the syllabus. It might seem silly to have a quiz on something so basic as a syllabus, but this professor was drilling it into our heads that the syllabus is important in preparation for class—essential, really. As you can probably guess, reading the syllabus was not one of my priorities that first week, and I absolutely bombed that first quiz. I left the classroom in complete shock—having failed my first test in college. That this should have been an easy few points made my shock even worse. I pouted for awhile, maybe ate some comfort food, and then determined *never* to let an easy quiz—or anything else—slide by.

That was Part I of my three-week whiplash.

Now comes Part II.

I sat down and worked out a study schedule that was really quite impressive...on paper. With only a few minutes here and there for eating and bathroom breaks, I planned to be in one of three states: in class, studying, or sleeping (for my allotted five hours of sleep). I even allowed myself a half-hour each weekend for leisure or maybe a quick ski trip to the mountains. When I completed the schedule, I dramatically capped my pen and opened my books, proud of myself for being such a responsible college student.

I spent the next few days of college trying to follow this plan. Before long, I found—*surprise!*—that it was impossible. Maybe it was impossible for me. Maybe it was impossible for anyone. But I knew it wouldn't work. I found myself burning out after only a few *days*. I knew my class notes very, very well, but I no longer cared. Soon, I wasn't paying attention in class, and I teetered on the verge of complete exhaustion. I realized what was happening, so I backed off and abandoned this insane schedule. I then overcompensated for my near-burnout and began not studying enough. I floundered for a few days until I decided: *I need a real schedule.* A plan. One just for me.

Everyone is different and will prefer studying at different times of the day and in different ways, but *schedules* are important. College requires a great deal of thinking, and each day will bring more and more assignments and concepts for you to make sense of. And once you graduate, you'll need the power of schedules to handle an even tougher study schedule—or a real, live workload, such as one that comes with a job. A schedule will help you focus your energy on what you are learning and waste less energy on deciding what to do each day.

Your schedule must be your own. *You* have to live it, so make sure you can.

SLEEP

Sleep is an essential aspect of your schedule. You might think you'll zoom past all your classmates with a mere five hours of sleep, but chances are the only zooming that will occur will be that nauseating sensation inside your brain that accompanies fatigue. You almost certainly won't be able to keep up if you keep a poor sleep schedule.

Studies show that students who get a good night's sleep perform better than those who don't. Don't believe me? Well, it took me a very long time before I realized the power of sleep. It was in the middle of my first year of law school. I was just like many of you—staying up late for just about any reason and then sleeping in until just before class. Well, you might be able to fake your way through as an insomniac—but the deeper you get into college, the higher the stakes and the harder it is to correct bad habits.

One day I realized just how awful I felt and how poorly I was doing because I was so sleep-deprived. That, combined with the bad study schedule, convinced me to be more strategic about this basic element.

Imagine how much better you could do if your brain were functioning correctly. That's right. Your brain simply cannot work as effectively—remember Habit #1? ("Make Your Study Efficient and Effective")—when you don't get enough sleep. Sure, there might be the occasional late-night party. Of course, some might need a bit more than eight hours (long sleepers), while others can get by and *stay* fully alert with less (short sleepers). There are also those who are night owls (late sleepers) and those who are early birds (early sleepers). We're just learning about these differences, but what researchers do know is that these differences…make a difference.

For us, the danger is for two groups: The first group includes those who think they can cheat sleep for an extended period. Sure, you can get by on less than you need—but only for so long. And the older you get, the less able you are to do this for even short periods. So this is a bad habit to start relying on.

The second group is composed of those who are significantly long sleepers—some might need nine hours a night, or even more, which does cut into study time—and late sleepers. Many classes and exams are, after all, in the mornings. If you're a long *and* late sleeper, then you're going to need to think even more carefully about your schedule. You'll still have lots of studying to do, and you'll need to be even more efficient, as you'll have comparatively less time in which to do it.

Need more convincing? Researchers assert that a lack of sleep leads to (1) an inability to concentrate; (2) impaired memory; and (3) decreased physical performance.[1] Persistent sleep deprivation can cause drastic mood swings and even hallucinations. Without an opportunity to rest and regenerate, our brain gradually loses its ability to function at an optimal level, and then at all.

On the positive side, consistent sleep allows the body and brain to repair themselves, grow, and make neural connections, which can be used to speed and reinforce learning; "nerve-signaling patterns" that occur during the day, while people are awake, can be mirrored and repeated during sleep. These nerve-signaling repetitions help encode data, information, and memories—all while affecting the ability to think. To *learn*.

There is, if you're still skeptical, a direct link between sleep and academic performance. Students who perform at higher levels in school with greater academic success share a common habit: they adopt regular sleep habits to allow their brains time to rest and grow.

This makes basic sense and pretty much speaks for itself. Not getting enough sleep affects your ability to perform mental and physical tasks. At some point sleep deprivation becomes a serious issue. Yet students seem to revel in sleep deprivation!

Getting enough sleep improves your mental and physical abilities. We really don't have to read study after study to know this is true; we live it. When you get enough sleep, your mind is able to perform at its peak. When you don't, it's harder to stay conscious, let alone to undergo (and actually remember) intense study.

Yes, it seems crazy that many students deprive themselves of something so basic when the benefits are so obvious, and as students, we simply cannot afford to have our brains functioning below their peak level. We *need* our brains!

Why so much on sleep?

Here's why: you should consider putting those late-night cramming sessions behind you. If that's what everyone else is doing—that's no reason for *you* to do so as well. Get your sleep! If you develop a pattern of being fully awake during the day, and of sleep-

---

1   See NINDS, or the National Institute of Neurological Disorders and Stroke, in "Brain Basics: Understanding Sleep."

ing consistently and fully, you will feel better and perform better in college.

EXERCISE

During my first year of college I saw my classmates, and myself, slowly pack on more and more weight—what is commonly referred to as the "Freshman 15." As a result of sitting all day with little or no exercise, the weight seemed to just stick to us. And, as with the section above, the effects of being suddenly overweight were alarming. Schedule a block of exercise at least several times a week. This is almost as important as getting enough sleep. It keeps you from being sedentary, gets your blood moving, and helps you be more alert.

Recently, a 26-year-old guy from India set a record for playing *Grand Theft Auto IV.* He played for forty hours straight, and claimed that he was able to maintain his stamina because he exercised regularly.[2] It might seem strange that being physically fit helps with an activity where you sit down and move your thumbs to control a video game, but staying fit keeps your blood moving and allows you to stay alert. Your study sessions are actually similar to playing video games: they both involve sitting in one place for extended periods of time and moving your fingers. I wouldn't recommend studying for forty hours, but you get the point.

Exercise improves your stamina. Much of the time, college is an endurance test. You *need* that stamina.

In addition to stamina, exercise will help in an additional area of some importance: you'll not only feel better, you'll look better. Is it worth pointing out that this can make a very, very, very big difference in your social life?

If you still have a hard time justifying exercise when you could be studying, try recording your outlines into audio files and listen while you exercise, or take note cards while you go for a walk. Honestly, you shouldn't feel that you need to study *all* the time— that's a sign that you're being neither efficient nor effective.

---

2   Apparently the record was broken in 2010 by more than fifteen hours—by a swim coach who cited regular exercise as well. That record wasn't official, but even so....

Learning all of the concepts in all of your courses, and doing all the required work, is challenging but doesn't take *all* of your time.

If you still feel like you are cutting too much into your study time, try this: write down everything you do during the day and the amount of time it takes to accomplish each activity. You will find more than enough time to exercise—and you won't have to cut anything out. Finding time for exercise forces you to be more efficient in your other activities and to make the most out of everything you do.

We do what's important. Exercise is important.

EATING

Make sure you schedule time for three healthy meals every day. This might seem silly, but it's amazingly easy to get side-tracked. You might think that if you read just one more assignment, or cross-check just one more reference, or grab a bite while reading, or hang out for just a little while longer, it won't make a difference. But it *will* make a difference, in a bad way, if your blood sugar keeps bouncing from binge highs to near-comatose lows. This is no way to study.

I found that if I set aside twenty minutes to eat three times a day, set aside my notes, and then ate a healthy meal or snack, I was able to return to my studies more refreshed than if I tried to "study" while I ate.

Of course, some people are different. Some might need four or even five smaller meals a day. (Those who exercise regularly find this energizing—and a good way to lose weight. That's right. More, smaller meals lead to weight loss.) Again, do what is best for you, but do not try to get by on just two or even just one meal a day.

The point of scheduling times to sleep, exercise, and eat well is to stay healthy. Staying healthy is good for your brain. If you stick to your eating plan, you will be healthier, more alert, and more able to focus on and absorb the material when you do study. These will contribute to better overall performance, even if the actual time spent studying is slightly less. This is being effective *and* efficient—which takes us right back to Habit #1 ("Make Your Study Efficient and Effective").

Aside from scheduling times during the day to eat, it is important that what you put into your body is good for you. Maintain a *healthy* diet. Sure, lots of students eat lots of junk food, and that's fine on occasion (such as *after* finals). For the rest of the time, however, when you're trying to maintain the energy and stamina to stay intensely focused for extended periods of time, it is better to eat healthy foods that are high in energy but low in "junk." Sugary, oily, and caffeine-packed foods might give you that immediate boost of energy, but the crash comes soon after. And overall you will begin to feel awful. If you're carrying just a few extra pounds—which also comes with eating junk food—you're going to start feeling *really* awful. You'll find yourself consuming more and more sugar and caffeine just to maintain that "boost." This adversely affects your heart, health, and brain—not to mention your self-image and social life. You'll feel even more stress—and you'll have less and less stamina to deal with the everyday stresses of college. Break this bad cycle.

Unfortunately for most of us, as members of the caffeine generation, we consume *way* too much caffeine. I'm probably not far off when I say that most students can't get through the day without a few Red Bulls and maybe a latté or three—and I won't lie by saying that I am not among you. The trick is to eat energy-rich food and give up short-term "fake" foods. Remember the guy who set the world record for the longest session of *Grand Theft Auto IV?* He cited not only exercise as essential to his extended performance, but also avoiding caffeine and sugar. He ate *figs* instead. And he was clearly able to push to higher levels of endurance. Now, I'm not a huge fan of figs, but there's still an important lesson here.

Eating better = performing better. As a student, you'll rely *very* seriously on your performance. Make sure the foods you feed your body and mind are healthy and provide real energy.

STUDY

Set aside blocks of time to study. I learned better when I studied for 30-60 minutes. Then I would take a break for 15 minutes. Yes, it's possible to "study" for 11 hours straight, collapse for a few hours of sleep, and then do it all over again the next day—but that's not an effective long-term strategy. You'll burn out long before finals.

As to a one-size-fits-all, "best" schedule…there probably isn't one.

30 minutes, 60 minutes, 90 minutes?

5-minute breaks, 15 minutes, one hour?

Do what works better for you, and perhaps test alternatives—but set aside times to study, and *stick to them,* every day.

Pick a spot to study, and return to it *every day.* This area could be in your school's library, in a common (but quiet) study area, or at your desk. Wherever is a good place for you. Many seem to prefer their neighborhood Starbucks or other café, but for reasons mentioned above and for the need not to be distracted, this is not the best choice, or even a good choice.

Returning to the same place to study is a good habit because when you sit down in your special study area, your brain automatically starts to get geared for studying. Your brain is an amazing thing, and it remembers and attributes different activities to different places. Everything in your study area will trigger a response in your brain that says, "Okay, now it is time to study." In your study place it is time to start thinking about learning—and that's all right, because "this is my study area."

Along with this, you should avoid studying in places where you do other things, which can confuse the parts of your brain devoted to studying. For example, studying in your bed right before sleep is a bad habit because your bed is for *sleep.* (Well, mostly.) When you climb into bed, your mind starts to shut down for the night; you've been setting this habit for twenty-plus years. By studying in bed, your brain will start associating your bed with thinking, not sleeping. This leads to a more difficult time getting to sleep *and* a less effective time studying, which leads to being more tired during the day and eventually to higher stress levels all around. Your life, as you know it, will end.

Joking aside, I once heard advice to allow at least an hour between study sessions and going to bed. Before hearing this advice, I was reading my textbooks in bed right before sleeping, and having a difficult time—not only in focusing on the material, but also unwinding and falling asleep after I stopped "studying." I took this advice, and solved one major problem with my study habits then and there. Since then, I get more out of studying *and* a better night's sleep.

DOWNTIME

I take my downtime in small segments during my study blocks. Others take their downtime on the weekend, in the evenings, or for extended periods during the day. Be wary, however, as both efficiency and effectiveness can be affected by excessive downtime. Only plan enough downtime to keep your mind fresh and your life balanced: don't overdo it.

I knew students who would attend class in the morning and then play video games all afternoon. At about 7:00 p.m., they would crack open their books. Needless to say, they were not at the top of the class and are thus not the kind of students we want to emulate, especially when the job market turns bad. Too much downtime will eventually overtake your studies. You are in college to learn—so take only enough of a break during your intense study sessions to keep you refreshed and, well, sane. College is about endurance, and you should think of it as a marathon, not a sprint. You *will* have to stick to extended hours of studying, which will come from (and then reinforce) your growing endurance.

The good news is that, with a realistic but intense study plan, you will be able to take off for longer periods—an afternoon, a day, or a weekend—and not have to worry. Downtime is qualitative as well as quantitative. The important point is that you're only balancing the need to relax with the need to study if you're doing both.

Another distraction comes with pre-study rituals. My (bad) habit often consisted of checking email a few times, updating Facebook, re-checking email to make sure no wild news or gossip would escape my immediate attention, reading interesting stories (and some not-so-interesting stories), and searching the web for things I wasn't even particularly interested in. We all get sucked into these little distractions and put off our chores, such as work, study, and taking out the trash—so no one is immune.

You will do better simply to jump into your studies. Save a few minutes, after you've accomplished some real learning, for some mindless distraction later. This is a challenge, and you need to be firm with yourself. If not, you end up wasting a *lot* of time, getting tired *and* bored before you even crack open your textbooks—and you won't get much out of it when you do study. This is one area where you can force yourself, fairly simply, to change a bad habit into a good one. When you study...*study!* Close your email. Close Facebook. Close everything that's not related to what you're doing at that moment: studying. This is a basic issue of time management, and it's exactly what you'll need once you start studying for finals, not to mention graduate school or your first professional job.

These little rituals aren't all bad—in moderation—if they help relax your mind before studying. What tends to happen, though, is that you get used to your mind wandering and want to avoid the intense focus of study. This takes us back to the bad habit that you need to change to a good habit.

If you need a break between classes or study sessions, give yourself a set number of minutes to relax—and then jump back in! For example, if you say, "I'm going to take a ten-minute break," then force yourself not to lie: set a timer. Do whatever you want for ten minutes, and when your timer chimes, get back to work.

As painful as this can sometimes be, you'll end up *enjoying* your downtime, because you will appreciate each minute, because you will have the satisfaction of honest studying, and because you won't feel guilty for taking that break.

BE FLEXIBLE, BUT STICK TO THE PLAN

A schedule is important because it allows you to make a plan and then forget about *planning* the plan. If you make up your mind about how you spend each day, then you do not have to worry about how each day will play out.

Things come up, sure. I am in law school with a family, so things come up more often than not—and you just have to adjust. This doesn't prove that planning is pointless; in fact it proves the opposite. The less you have to worry about each day, the more able you are to adjust when something does come up.

Likewise, be honest. If you aren't studying enough, or if you are burning out too early, adjust to a better balance. And then stick to the schedule.

9

USE WHAT YOU NEED TO SUCCEED

I learned many things too late in college. Among these was the value and benefit of the resources available to every college student.

The resource that I did use was the university's writing center. It's probably obvious that I enjoy writing, and one resource that helps me with my writing is the ability to talk with someone else about it. That someone else can read one of my papers—which were almost weekly exercises as a philosophy major—and that person can tell me what he or she liked (or didn't like), what made sense, and what was a total pile of, well, mismatched and ambiguous platitudes. (Some may argue, however, that all papers by philosophy majors are total piles of mix-matched and ambiguous platitudes, but that isn't exactly the point here.) The writing center provided an opportunity to have an objective expert read what I had written and provide suggestions—an invaluable service. And it didn't stop there—they helped me edit my papers and polish them to a far higher level than had I just submitted them to the professors as (in truth) drafts.

Seems too good to be true, you say? Well, consider this: your university *wants* you to succeed. That may not seem a realistic goal of theirs, but in reality it is. They want you to succeed because your success is like an advertisement, not only in how you might interact with other prospective students, but also (and in many ways more important) in how you present yourself to everyone else, including employers and anyone who might have an opinion about the quality of their graduates. When your quality goes up, both in school and in your career, the school's reputation goes up. If your quality is not what it should be, that reflects poorly on the entire university—and is a serious concern of administrators.

Thus, your school will provide you with everything they possibly can to make sure that you are learning to the best of your ability—it is in their best interest for you to get the help you need. Here's another point to consider: you are *paying* for these resources. So you might as well take advantage of them...and succeed in the process.

Not only that, but the writing center and other university resources are built on readily available and renewable resources. When I was using the writing center, it was upperclassmen who were helping me. When I was an upperclassman, I worked in the writing center, doing exactly what other students had helped me with when I'd just started out. This is what universities bank on— the fact that all those who enjoy writing will stick together and help others. The same goes for math, science, you name it. Every department at your school will have labs and tutorials of some type available for everyone who is taking a class or needs help in particular areas. To make the most of your education, you *need* to use these resources. Make it a habit.

HABIT #13: USE UNIVERSITY RESOURCES

While it would be impossible for me to provide an exhaustive list of all the resources available at each college or university, of course, I'd like to point out just a few that are most helpful and most readily available. Some may seem self-explanatory, yet you would be surprised by how many students don't know that the resources exist, or if they do know, choose not to use them.

Also, as you get into your chosen major and when you're more aware of the resources available to you, you will find many other degree-specific resources and opportunities to maximize your learning (and thus grades and success) during college.

Use these resources.

LIBRARY

The library is the university's hub—much more so than high school or elsewhere. It is so important that most schools require students to take tours of the library or attend some sort of library orientation. Go. Learn the library, and learn about its resources. In particular, meet the librarians. They can be a fantastic resource for finding esoteric sources when you need them.

You might think, by the way, that the internet has made librarians—and the library—obsolete. Not so. There's so much out there that it's even *more* important to know how to get it—and professors will be sensitive to the *quality* of sources you're using. Librarians are expert at helping you get these. You will soon be grateful that you went and learned as much as you could.

In the library you will obviously find a large array of books, but you will also find computer labs, information about everything that the university offers, and a library staff knowledgeable in helping students. Most libraries will even have departments that coincide directly with your major. Go through the section of the library that pertains to your section. Learn the ins and outs and content-specific resources available. Librarians are smart and caring. They can help you more than you know—and they actually *like* research challenges.

Something else to consider is this: while the internet is a massive, invaluable resource, it does not have all the information you need, and it definitely does not have all of the high-quality information you need. Sometimes, the answers you are looking for are found in obscure, out-of-print books that are hidden on the shelves, or are available only via an interlibrary loan. While fine-tuning your internet research skills, don't lose the skills required to sift through actual books and journals to find what you are looking for.

PROFESSORS

As discussed, getting to know your professors and using them as resources outside of class time is important to your success. Another part of this is that the better the relationship you have with your professors (on a professional level, of course) the more likely they are to write a stellar recommendation for you later. Get to know them, and they can be an invaluable resource for your graduate school plans and even well into your career.

I got to know one professor very well. One of the last things he told me before I left college was that he would continue to be available. I have stayed in contact with him and with several other professors through the years, and they have been *very* important in providing guidance and help.

Teaching Assistants

Many professors have research and teaching assistants who can also be great resources. They have access to the professors and know their academic and other preferences. They can point you in the right direction on assignments and exams, sometimes more so than professors (because they're the ones grading them). Also, professors are thinking of the class as a whole. If one bit of important information goes to one student (based on that student's insightful question), professors are likely to share that with everyone. Assistants, on the other hand, are usually helping the student before them at a given moment. This leads to information that might be more useful than you would get without taking the effort to confirm a specific point.

Keep in mind too that the assistant is smart, very smart, and is usually deeply involved in the subject as an upperclassman or (more likely) as a graduate student. As such, they will be able to help you think through problems or help you better understand less-than-easily understood concepts. That's something that cannot be shared except by actually wanting the help...and doing something to get it.

Review Sessions

I wish, badly, that I had taken advantage of these more in college. It wasn't until I got to law school that I really started attending review sessions, and they are beyond helpful.

More often than not, a professor will give the students a totality of information that is far greater than they can put in the exam—and rightfully so, as there is simply too much information in any given subject to fit into one exam. Review sessions are important because they narrow the focus for you. Even if only slightly, this narrowing is highly beneficial.

The review session will go over things that will be on the test, and is another opportunity for you to ask questions, get the most out of class, and ultimately, be well prepared for the final.

Take advantage of these sessions. If you don't have time, then *make* the time. Attend the review sessions for each of your classes.

STUDENT ORGANIZATIONS

There are hundreds of student organizations, of all types, sizes, and charters. There's a group for virtually every subject you will learn in college, and even more for extracurricular activities. The academic groups are filled with students interested in that particular subject, of course—but also with numerous activities that round out the academics. A group might invite guest speakers, organize trips, coordinate with faculty, you name it.

For example, one of the student organizations I joined was focused on screenwriting. I was interested in screenwriting, and the group not only read and discussed screenplays, but each member brought to the table a unique perspective that helped the group as a whole. Several members had never written (or even read) a screenplay, and they were able to benefit by the shared, greater experience of those of us who had. Not that we were "experts," but we shared an interest and were working to develop our skills in that area.

While it is good to join an organization such as this when you are interested, it might be even more helpful to join a group that focuses on a subject in which you are having a difficult time. For example, I went to several meetings for the university math society, which was filled with graduate students in mathematics and undergraduates who were leaning toward math as a career. I didn't actually join the group, but I went several times and met members who were easily able to help me when I had questions.

Find a directory of the student organizations on your campus. Talk with upperclassmen or professors about these organizations. Even if you don't join, you can attend meetings and get to know those who are members and benefit from their expertise.

This is social as well, of course. These can become meaningful friendships, sometimes lasting a lifetime. In college, we are all in the same boat, together, and most other students are willing to help.

STUDENT CENTERS

The writing center discussed above is an example of the many student centers you will find on campus. I also frequented the math labs, where teaching assistants were amazingly helpful.

A roommate of mine worked in the biology lab, and while I didn't ever go, knowing my roommate made me aware of how much help was available for anyone studying biology. Similarly, my wife worked in the genetics lab. At both places a student could walk in just about any time during the day and get the help needed for class, a research assignment, and even personal projects.

These labs are part of what you are paying for with your tuition—so take advantage of them. And take advantage of them *early*. Don't wait until the week before finals. They are students too, and they have their own finals to study for.

MISCELLANEOUS

All through college (and even now), I was interested in filmmaking. One feature I loved about my university was its multimedia lab. The lab had banks of state-of-the-art computers with the best film-editing software available. You could do just about anything in that lab, from animation and CGI to music recording and graphic design, and there was always someone there who knew how to use the equipment and help those who were just learning.

In doing research for this book, I found that most colleges and universities have similar labs devoted to making films or other media-related projects. There are so many "hidden" resources at universities, many of which are hidden simply because no one bothers to find them.

Search!

Make it a habit to actively search out the resources that you are paying for. And then *use* them. Think about what you like, and then find the resources. Or, find help for the subjects you need help in. Find what is available for your use, before you need it. The examples above are only a sampling of the many resources that can be found on campuses—all devoted to helping you.

10

Work Now, Play Later

We all remember the story of the ant and the grasshopper. The grasshopper played all summer long while the ant worked at setting aside food. When winter came, the ant survived because he had food, and the grasshopper died a horrible and slow death of starvation and exposure. Maybe the story you were told had a gentler ending, but when you're a college student, reality is harsh. Getting bad grades will *severely* hinder your future. Bad habits of procrastination and too much play are among the culprits.

HABIT #14: WORK NOW, PLAY LATER

Procrastination is a problem that plagued me throughout high school and college. I would get an assignment in class and swear up and down that I would finish the assignment well before it was due so that I could make changes and polish my work to a level near perfection. Nearly always, even with these good intentions, I would later wonder why I was staying up for forty-eight hours straight to finish a project. The end result was never what it could have been had I paced myself and spent time earlier working on the assignment. Worse, I *knew* this, and had only myself to blame. Despite telling myself that the hastily assembled project was my best work, I knew the truth.

Even while I was "playing"—goofing off, really—I also knew in the back of my mind that I had schoolwork to do, so I could never fully let go and actually *enjoy* the leisure time. It was a Catch-22, where I wasn't getting things done *and* I wasn't enjoying extracurricular activities to the fullest. Thankfully, I was able to get my head on straight toward the end of my time as an undergraduate and made concerted efforts to finish assignments before they were due. In law school, this became a requirement, not just a "good practice."

Procrastination was hardly unique to me. This hinders most students. We have the best intentions, largely because we know deep down that college is good for us—and we might even enjoy the project. I was in a screenwriting class one semester, doing something that I absolutely loved (and still love), yet I *still* had issues with putting assignments off. Maybe it was the fact that I lived less than half an hour away from some of the best ski slopes in the world, or maybe it was those college parties everyone hears about, but I simply didn't make the time to finish projects and assignments in advance of their due date. The result was *always* something less than it could have been.

Finally, after many failed attempts to overcome procrastination, I decided simply that if I was in college, I was going to do college to the best of my ability. I made a goal to make a daily schedule for everything I had to do, including a well-paced schedule for finishing large projects well ahead of their due dates, and I promised myself that I would do everything on my daily schedule before doing anything else. And when I say anything else, I mean *everything* else: I didn't watch TV, play games, read books, hang with friends, chill with my girlfriend...I did nothing until my work was done.

I had a few missteps, of course, but it mostly worked—and I found that the quality of my schoolwork increased greatly. Because I naturally wanted to be doing things other than studying and finishing assignments, I made the time to get everything done that pertained to school as early in the day as possible, freeing up the rest of the day for whatever I needed to get done (or just wanted to do).

Crucially, there was another benefit: I found, to my surprise, that once I buckled down to get the work done, I could actually get the work done faster than I thought I could, so I was actually *not* spending that much more time! I was getting high-quality work done, earlier, *and* I was able to watch TV, play games, read books, hang with friends, and chill with my girlfriend. This is the *efficiency* part of being effective and efficient.

The trick is to schedule easily manageable chunks of work to do each day—then finish every item on your list before you tackle anything else. If your list includes items that are too broad, such as "Do 25-page paper" and "Study ch. 4-8 in Sociology," then your list is not sufficiently precise. Instead, write "draft outline for paper *x* by Monday noon." That's something that *can* be done, allowing you to move on to the next item, perhaps "Study ch. 4 in Sociology."

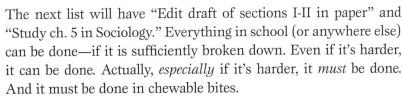

The next list will have "Edit draft of sections I-II in paper" and "Study ch. 5 in Sociology." Everything in school (or anywhere else) can be done—if it is sufficiently broken down. Even if it's harder, it can be done. Actually, *especially* if it's harder, it *must* be done. And it must be done in chewable bites.

You should take it one step at a time. You will succeed.

Make it a habit to work now and play later. Not only will your school work improve, but you'll also be able to produce high-quality, time-intensive projects. You will enjoy your "play" even more, knowing that after working hard and making real progress, you really *can* play…without guilt.

As an important side note, it's useful to emphasize just how much everything in your college career will stick with you for the rest of your life, and especially for your early career. It's not that you'll walk around your retirement villa boasting about your GPA (or at least I hope not), but it is true that how well you do in college will make a difference to your graduate school prospects and in your efforts to secure your first professional job, whether or not you do go on to graduate school first. These are highly interdependent: admissions committees and recruiters both care about grades, not just for the grades themselves but more deeply for what they represent. Each individual grade, while not vital in and of itself, contributes to your GPA. Your GPA, because it is important in getting that first job or getting into graduate school, is a piece of the whole pie and will play a part in determining your future.

I, for example, am not a top student when it comes to math (which might be one reason I chose to go to law school), but I was determined to take math classes that satisfied a goal of mine: to master the concepts of math. While my aspirations were noble, the results were like a swift kick to the behind—and not just once. With each grade that was not what I'd hoped for (nor in line with my other grades), my determination only grew. I kept taking those classes…and ended up not becoming a master mathematician. Give me an A for effort, but the point is that I did not get an "A" in those classes. This brought my GPA down.

While I was a top student in other courses, my successes were tainted because of my insistence on mastering mathematics. Those grades in math further made it more difficult to go to the law school

I wanted to attend—I had to work extra hard in other areas to make up for my less-than-perfect GPA. Not to mention the time that I wasted doing classes that I had no interest in and that did nothing but make me miserable. My point is that these math courses, while seemingly unimportant, had lasting effects and made life more difficult when I was trying to look my best on law school applications.

I'd like to offer a side note to this: I did learn important math concepts, and these are important in life. What I might have done, instead, was to pay attention to something I felt, which is repeated above: "I had no interest in math, which made me miserable."

We *should* challenge ourselves in college, but it should be in meaningful ways that are of genuine interest to us. So, perhaps I might have found physics, or astronomy, or geometry interesting and within my grasp. If so, I would have gained knowledge *and* kept a stellar GPA *and* impressed law schools *and* actually had a better time.

It gets worse for those who are headed into a profession, and in particular law. For example, when trying to get your license to practice law, you have to apply to a state's Bar Association, or "Bar." The Bar will take a *very* detailed look into your past to see if your character and fitness meet the standards of what the Bar thinks a lawyer should be. A friend of mine is a top-notch law student, doing everything in law school exactly as he should. He got amazing grades and landed a spectacular internship with a national law firm, but was delayed more than *eight months* because of some foolish decisions in college. This was eight months when he could have been making nearly ten times what he was making as a student, paying off student loans or saving for that yacht, but instead he spent those eight months working the same jobs he was working as a student.

You have to pass through similar character and fitness checks throughout your life, whether or not you are explicitly told that you and your past choices are being scrutinized. Just remember this: have fun, but do so in moderation. It's one thing to get buzzed and discuss the finer points of some pointless philosophical debate at 4:00 a.m.; it's another thing to do something that is, well, a criminal act. Unfortunately, college is overrun with a culture of excess, such as binge drinking—even when many students will say, privately, that they don't even really like alcohol. Do *not* feel pressured into doing things that could have serious consequences later on: from jail time, to drunkenly running people over, to unplanned pregnancy or STDs.

If you don't want to do something, don't do it. Do not do something for someone else's "validation." It's not worth it, and chances are high that they won't even remember you, much less remember what it was they were being validated for. You should be secure enough in your own ego that you can make choices and be comfortable with those choices. If they don't like that, that's their problem, not yours. You'll be amazed at how this attitude makes *you* a leader.

If you *do* want to do something, well, that's your choice. But you should still be careful. What you do in college will stick with you whether you like it or not; it's important to get used to the idea and be at least modestly responsible with your future.

11

KEEP LIVING LIFE

I've gone on and on about how important college is and how the habits you develop today will affect your future in meaningful and lasting ways. I have certainly tried to convey the importance of these few years, not only in securing an education but also setting up your career.

But don't take my word for it: any research will yield the simple truth that you are better off with a college degree than without—usually much better off. And the benefits are even greater if you do well. Sure, there are a few exceptions to the rule, in the same sense of Beethoven being deaf yet producing amazing music. With top grades in college, job security is better, pay is better, the level of comfort in your life is better, your stress levels are lower, and you ultimately have far more opportunities. A college degree opens doors. A high GPA opens them wider.

Yet for many (as for me), this is the first time that the axe meets the grinding stone. This is what I experienced: for the first time in my life, I actually had to *study* in order to get good grades. About halfway through college, I decided on law school, and so felt even more pressure to do well. This intensified the stress—my entire future seemed to weigh down on me.

In addition, I started a family by getting married and having two children. I got a full-time job, so in addition to that, college became the "added burden" rather than the main event. Those relationships were by far the most important—but college was important too. I loved devoting time to my family, but I also *had* to do well in college…for them as well as for me. This was difficult. I won't lie. And it was and still is common for people to wonder how I do it. When so much of your time is taken up for school and work, how is it possible to maintain *any* relationship, much less three?

Part of the answer is that we do what we must. More to the point, we become much more efficient when we *have* to be more efficient. Managing a heavier workload will lead to either better habits—or giving up. If we assume that the former is the better choice, these habits are written to help you manage the workload of college while still enjoying the personal side of life—and if you're single, imagine all that free time!

Another part of the answer is in balance, which leads us to our next principle and habit.

HABIT #15: KEEP LIVING LIFE

College is a vitally important time in your life. For four years (usually), you will learn and explore and grow. Done in the right spirit, these can be among the most exciting, enjoyable years in your life.

Looked at differently, however, it is *only* four years of an entire lifetime. Don't sacrifice relationships or burn the people who make you genuinely happy for the possibility of being successful (and, presumably, happy) later. Don't give up friendships, family, and happiness *now*.

The good news is that you don't have to. You *can* keep living your life, and you *should*. It makes for a better-rounded person; it rounds out your résumé; it helps in getting into graduate school; it helps in interviews with future employers; and it will help you *in* college. Consider this example: in an interview for a prestigious internship during law school, much of what the interviewers and I talked about was—you guessed it—my family! I got the internship and realized that those interviewing me were apparently interested in more than grades: they thought it was important to be balanced too.[3]

This is a good time to practice living a balanced life because, well, it doesn't get easier. We should learn how to deal with an overloaded plate not just because we like to work hard but also because we will continually have practical concerns and personal desires—and they might be in conflict. Plus, isn't it better to be successful *and* happy?

Efficiency is a large part of the answer. Yes, I've mentioned it many times, and I don't want to beat a dead horse, but…being effi-

3   This point is made in a book, *The Insider's Guide to Getting a Big Firm Job* (which I didn't see until after my interview), and which spells out just how different interviewers' perceptions are from students' generally mistaken beliefs. Although the book is geared more toward law students, it has some excellent advice about interviews, résumés, and techniques to find a job.

cient in your studies allows you to enjoy your life *and* be a better, more successful college student. Do the things that make you happy, maintain relationships, and just keep living life. Don't become so consumed with school that you forget who you are.

MANAGE YOUR STRESS

Stress can be horrible and debilitating, depending on how you let it affect you. Many college students have never experienced severe levels of stress; some find it difficult to handle, and some find it impossible. Counseling services (another common service available to college students) are filled with students suffering depression or even breakdown. Many struggle in all aspects of student life: trouble studying, trouble coping with looming assignments, trouble planning, trouble organizing, and difficulty transitioning to an independent lifestyle. College can be overwhelming, and personal issues such as the tumultuous love lives of many college students add substantially to the sense of being adrift.

Not everyone experiences this level of stress, of course, and not everyone handles stress well (or badly). The stress of college does exist, and you do need to learn how to deal with it. Stress can be objective, such as from coursework, complex theories, exhaustion, and assignments. Or it may be subjective, such as a sense of an overload of coursework, the inability to understand all of what you're trying to learn, a chronic lack of sleep, a sense of doom with those looming finals—or a difficult social life. As the parallel stresses make clear, how we deal with these stresses is at least as important as the stresses themselves. You should not feel bad about experiencing stress—but you *do* need to *deal* with the stress and take care of yourself. Sustained stress will inhibit your ability to perform to the best of your capabilities, which will, yes, only add more stress to your already over-stressed collegiate life.

The first thing to do is to pinpoint the source of your stress. Then fix it...or adjust to it. If nothing comes to mind, then sit down to identify the areas in your life that add to your workload. Anything and everything, from assignments to laundry. The act of sitting down and writing out these sources is therapeutic in itself: You are *doing something!* You realize there is a problem and you are identifying its source. Many times, the act of locating the source of stress is enough to avoid or at least moderate problems.

Once these sources are identified, try to eliminate or at least reduce the stress. For example, if you are having trouble understanding certain concepts, then add to your plan: commit to (1) visiting your professor regularly, with specific questions to clarify points you do not understand and recommendations for supplemental reading; (2) attending sessions with a teaching assistant or lab to go over general points in the subject so that you're absolutely certain you understand them; and (3) actually reading the supplemental material. This enables you to feel more confident that you're working toward a solution, and you will actually work toward that solution. While it might seem that you're adding to your workload, in fact you are not. You are going to spend your time studying in a more focused, more efficient way, and even time spent reading supplemental materials will be time you would have simply been stressing instead.

If you find, as a second example, that you don't have enough time during the day to accomplish what you need to do, then it's time to re-evaluate your schedule. You must prioritize and make time for what is *most* important. Simply identifying these issues and the specifics of your situation will, usually, be a major part of the solution. Many times we try to mask our stress without trying to resolve the problem—and typically these sources of stress are avoidable. Prioritizing is helpful in college and is an absolute must as you move into a career. So begin prioritizing now!

Even if the above solves the problem, you should still read about stress and stress-relief techniques, and maybe even see a counselor. These techniques are likely to work for you, both for college and afterwards. Stress comes from many directions, often without warning, and without a single standard of the "right" level of stress tolerance. It is thus a good idea to focus on reducing your stress, to increase your stress tolerance, and to have a plan for when high levels of stress do hit.

Here's how I handle it: when I am at school or in the middle of a project, I deal with stress by taking a power nap. If I'm in class, I focus on stretching the muscles in my feet, wiggling them around, and then looking forward to a power nap after the lecture. If at home, I take a bath or go for a short run. These techniques may seem silly, but they work, and I don't have nearly as much stress as I would if I didn't use these forms of relief. More important, I don't *feel* stressed. Consequently, I go into the classroom (or an exam room) with energy, not panic.

Do your research about relieving stress. A few quick searches on "stress relief tips" will pull up loads of advice on the web. Once you find something that works for you, use it. Then think about other ways to relieve other stresses.

DON'T OVERBURDEN YOURSELF

Part of living life and maintaining a healthy pace and balance through college is in not creating *additional* burdens. This is pretty much common sense, so I won't say more than a few words—but sometimes a few words is just the right number.

The start of college is not the time to make major life changes. We should be in a state of progression as individuals, true, constantly working to better ourselves. But college itself counts as a big progression, and it accounts for a lot of time and energy. Clear this hurdle, and *then* move on to another. Don't sacrifice your performance in school by trying to do too much at once.

I remember one point in college when I was working nearly sixty hours a week, writing a novel and several screenplays, trying to care for a pregnant wife—and then I decided I was looking a little chunky around the midsection and needed to lose weight. I was working at a movie theater, late into the night, and then going for a jog each morning before classes. I got about two hours of sleep each night and lived on energy drinks. Needless to say, I don't remember those months very well, and I'm pretty sure I was bordering on the brink of nervous breakdown.

Learn from my mistake. Don't load too much on your plate, and don't load *anything* extra on your plate that you don't have to—because it will already be full. Focus on who you are and what you have right now, and be the best you can be.

Habit #16: Maintain a Positive Attitude

College is hard, but it is also a fantastic opportunity. You get to spend several years to…*think*. How great is that?!

It is important to have fun. It is also important to engage in the process of learning and developing as a person and as a college student. Much of how well we can do these is in whether we want to.

College is a unique experience. It may well be the only time in your life that you study so many topics—and topics that *you* get to choose. It is a time where you can explore ideas, ask questions, and learn both philosophical and highly specific concepts. Many (perhaps most) college students don't take full advantage of this. I certainly didn't, at least during my first years. I was so caught up in getting good grades and doing homework that I forgot to *enjoy* college. (Obviously, it was easy to enjoy the skiing and the parties, but I'm talking about enjoying the actual *learning* part of college too.)

Never forget that college is a unique time to learn, and to learn how to enjoy the process of learning. Whatever your circumstances, this is a terrific time; an appreciation for just how lucky you are to be in college can help greatly in all of the other issues we've discussed…and more.

An Attitude of Success

This is an extension of having a positive attitude. The same principle applies. You need to be positive about yourself as a student as well as about your overall experience. If you see yourself as successful and fully capable of performing well on your exams (and if you follow through on the means to actually do well), you *will.*

There is an idea that a person is the physical depiction of his thoughts. You are what you think—and if you're thinking about being successful and having a fulfilling and worthwhile experience in college, then you will. Alternatively, if you are focused on the negative aspects of yourself as well as the many challenges of the college experience, you will likely not have an enjoyable time, nor will you perform as well as you could. Much of our performance is based on whether we *believe.*

Do you remember the children's story about the little train engine trying to reach the top of the mountain? Think like that little train, constantly telling yourself that you *know* you can do it. This is part of success: knowing that you are capable of success and then bringing that positive attitude—with all the good habits that it brings—into reality.

UNREALISTIC EXPECTATIONS

While you *are* aiming for an attitude of being a successful college student, you should not have unrealistic expectations about what "being a successful student" really means.

Being a successful college student entails doing the very best you can do. For most of us, this is a lot. It is certainly much more than many students *actually* achieve, which is sad. If you develop and apply the habits outlined in this book, you will do your best. You might not be at the number-one spot in your class, and you might not even be in the top ten percent of your class (although that is likely), but you will be successful if you did your best. There is only one #1 in your class, after all, and the competition is intense to get there. Moreover, that is not really the point—even if others (or you) think it is. Don't beat yourself up if you didn't do as well as you'd hoped, as long as you *truly* did your best. Your goal is to look back on your college school experience—each year, each semester, each course—and know that you did your best and got the most out of it, both in terms of actual learning and in terms of friendships, greater awareness, and fun.

If, by chance, you *haven't* done your best, then now is the time to change. Now! Dig in your heels a bit harder and put forth real effort. Your best. Your *very* best. When you do, you will be surprised at how much you can accomplish...and how minor all those old challenges now look.

I remember looking back on my first year—feeling a sense of accomplishment but also feeling that I could have done better. Upon thinking about it, I realized that I really had given it my best effort and had performed at the peak of my capability. With that I was happier and more satisfied. I realized later still that I'd become a better student and had drawn even more from the experience, both practically and in terms of really learning what I was study-ing. That's all you need. Do your best and you will do well in college, you will do well in your career, and your life will be better and more satisfying.

YOUR CLASSMATES

When aiming for that positive attitude, some of the worst hurdles are your classmates. These are the people you see every day, the people who will become your friends and colleagues, and ultimately the people you are competing against. It becomes difficult to maintain the positive attitude when others around you are complaining about how much work there is to do, how hard it is, blah, blah, blah. I don't think they're trying to psych you out with this kind of talk—well, most of them—but it kills a successful attitude. When others complain about how hard it is, it's easy to join in and wallow in self-pity. When you do this, it becomes more difficult to be motivated and to give your best effort (your "very best"!) every day.

The solution is to rise above conversations like this, and *do not participate.* You might think that everyone else is watching you or listening to what you have to say, or even hoping for agreement. Odds are they're not really paying that much attention; they're just miserable. As unfortunate as that is, you cannot let this affect (and infect) your own good attitude and habits. If it persists, you must decline to be a part of that group. Be friendly, of course, but don't join in the negativity.

Another attitude and motivation killer is when classmates discuss how *easy* college is! When you hear this, you're probably thinking, "What?! This is one of the hardest things I've ever done *in my life!* If it's easy for *them,* what's wrong with *me?*"

If you hear this, chances are games *are* being played. What to do? Again, do not join in a conversation like this. It's simply a no-win situation: you agree, you disagree, it doesn't matter. It's a pointless statement with no good result. Just know that everyone is working hard to keep up and everyone—really, everyone!—is nervous about the exams and grades and their futures, et cetera, et cetera.

Moreover, what you find easy or self-explanatory will be hard or downright obtuse for someone else. Likewise, topics others seem to pick up by osmosis you struggle with. (For example, math is still some illusive wizardry that I've never been able to grasp, but the metaphysical realities of Kant, Peirce—not a misprint—and Descartes make sense to me.) Subjects can be *hard*. You should not judge your own status or performance on conversations, nor should you even *listen* to them. They are distractions, and harmful distractions at that. You don't need any more distractions, so just don't. Know that you are doing your very best—and actually *do* your very best. Do not engage in or promote emotional gamesmanship; worry about yourself and loved ones instead.

I had one friend who would *never* talk about the exams. Not even two words. When the rest of us finished our exams and met outside the examination rooms to discuss the ups and downs of that particular exam, she would politely walk on by and completely avoid our conversations. I had other friends who would hound her about her thoughts on the exam. She would simply (but politely) refuse. At first I thought she was probably self-conscious about her performance and felt maybe she hadn't done all that well on the exams. As it turned out, she was one of the top students in my class; she did extremely well. She just didn't like to get freaked out, worried, or upset over something that did absolutely nothing toward her goal. We could do well to follow her lead by keeping our personal performance...personal.

More than this, our goals should not be to compete with others, but to compete with ourselves. Be the best you can be. Master your study habits to become more efficient and effective. As hard as it might be, forget about everyone else and how they are doing. Just do your best. Your very best.

COLLEGE IS NOT FOREVER

About two years into my college experience (and after several difficult courses and some personal drama that nearly everyone encounters at some point in college), I felt I had been in college for an eternity. I found it hard to believe that this kind of abuse could go on for another two years. I pushed through, and when I look back on the experience, it feels like a dream. Seriously, the entire experience goes by so fast that we often forget to stop and enjoy what we're doing.

We want to do well in life, whether we aspire to become a CEO, doctor, dentist, attorney, professor, or whatever else. College is a means to an end, but it should also be an end in itself: a time to be enjoyed. After all, you've worked hard to get to this point, and your career isn't going to make life easier—so enjoy the time in college, and remember that it won't last forever. Enjoy it while you can.

PERFORMANCE ON EXAMS

Your performance on exams can go one of three ways: you will have done well and will be pleased; you won't have done so well and will be unhappy; or you'll hit somewhere in the middle, and be mostly unhappy. When I use words like "well," or "not so well," these are relative to your best potential performance. If you got a "B" on an exam, and you know you did everything you could have done, then you did well. On the other hand, if you got a "B" and you know, deep down, that there was more you could have done, that you could have been a little more effective with your study time, then use this as lesson. Be honest with yourself, and use your honesty to do better—*your very best!*—in the future.

If you're still at the beginning of your time in college, realize that your first set of exams does *not* determine your status as a student or even how well you will do throughout college. These are your first college exams, and you should consider them a series of practice sessions. This is not to say that you shouldn't do your best, nor is to say that those grades are without consequences. The point is that you should learn from this experience *no matter what grades you receive.* You should analyze which classes you did well in and how your study for that class differed from your study for other classes. Although your exams do each label you with a grade, they provide additional insight to you as a student and how you can do better.

If you did well, good for you. Don't get over-confident, though. I saw many friends who aced the first round of exams and then bombed the next round because they became over-confident. If you did well in the first round, you are in a good place and of course

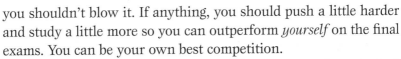

you shouldn't blow it. If anything, you should push a little harder and study a little more so you can outperform *yourself* on the final exams. You can be your own best competition.

If you hit somewhere in the middle—not great but not bad either—it is time to step it up. You got an "A" or two and a "B" or three and maybe even a "C + " or worse. This is the time to look at why you did well in some classes and why you didn't do as well in others. Use the grades to learn and then do better. Apply the better skills and develop the better habits. Aim for (and hit) better grades in *all* of your classes next time.

I know several friends who got excellent grades on their first exams and say they wish they had *not* done so well. No joke. They would tell me that because of their great early grades, they lost steam and became complacent and lax in their studies. If you didn't do as well on your exams, use this to boost your performance relative to those who aren't working as hard—or as efficiently.

We're all human; we all have bad days. If you had bad days on the days of the exams—or perhaps bad habits before the exams—realize this, "own" this, and dedicate yourself to doing better. Remind yourself that you have made it through the rigors of getting *into* college—you can use that same energy to do well *in* college.

If you bombed your exams, then you really need to re-evaluate your habits. Yes, I know we've discussed good study habits *ad nauseam,* but in the end it comes down to how well (or poorly) you use your time. Only *you* can decide to be better, and the truth is this: if you're serious about college, then you *can* improve your results…by improving your habits. Start by making short, attainable goals and work your way into a strong, sustainable study routine.

Regardless of how you did on the first set of exams, use your grades as a motivation builder. Keep your attitude positive. Your first semester is only one-eighth of your college experience. However you did, take lessons to prepare to do even better.

POSITIVE ATTITUDE, ONE MORE TIME

If you make an effort to enjoy your time in college, you will love it. Learning whatever you're learning won't be quite so hard, and your time won't be quite so stressful. So enjoy it, and have fun.

You have fun when *you* make it fun. Don't wait for someone else to make it fun for you. All of this is encompassed in having a good attitude. My dad used to say (much to my constant exasperation) that "your *attitude* determines your *altitude.*"

As the saying goes, the older I get, the smarter he gets. That mantra is true in most instances: your attitude *does* determine how well you do, how successful you are, and most important, how you grow and progress.

EPILOGUE

So that's it! A handful of essential habits that will help you attain your goals as a college student, including truly enjoying the times when you can kick back without worrying.

Not only will you do well on your exams, but you'll also have more time to be you, to do the things you love, to have fun—all the while being a successful college student who does well on exams and who is the presence in class everyone wants to befriend.

The idea is to start attaining these habits as soon as possible, prior to and during your very first week of college. If you're reading this book after your first week—or anytime in college, for that matter—it's not too late to use these habits to achieve your goals, to be effective, to use your time as a student as efficiently as possible, and to look back on your college time and...smile.

As you prepare for your college adventure, I'll offer just a few final words:

Best of luck to you!

About the Author

Derrick Hibbard placed in the top 15% of his first-year class and as a Dean's honor student at the University of Miami School of Law. Among other law school accomplishments, he received the CALI Award for highest grade in Property Law.

He graduated with high honors from Brigham Young University, earning a degree in Philosophy. He tutored and coached students in both high school and college; worked with Habitat for Humanity; and spent time working in an orphanage and school in Lusaka, Zambia.

Besides pursuing a legal career, Hibbard is an amateur filmmaker, screenwriter, and novelist. He is also author of *Law School Fast Track: Essential Habits for Law School Success.*

INDEX

OTHER BOOKS

LAW SCHOOL FAST TRACK: ESSENTIAL HABITS FOR LAW SCHOOL SUCCESS,
by Derrick Hibbard
ISBN: 978-1-888960-24-2, 93 pages,
US$12.95

For a law student, massive assignments loom
from the very first day—with no let-up until
final exams—and with zero feedback until
those finals. This book focuses on the *essential*
habits for your very first week of law school.
This book cuts right to the most important issues. Better success, easier
study, and higher grades and graduation prospects.

LAW SCHOOL UNDERCOVER: A VETERAN PROFESSOR TELLS THE TRUTH
ABOUT ADMISSIONS, CLASSES, CASES, EXAMS, LAW
REVIEW AND MORE,
by Professor "X"
ISBN 978-1-888960-15-0, 149 pages,
US$16.95

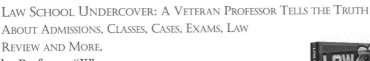

Written by a 20-year veteran law professor,
this book covers the most important aspects of
law school, from selecting the right law school
to admissions to first year to law review, moot court, and though graduation and jobs. Offers students the straight truth they will get nowhere
else.

JAGGED ROCKS OF WISDOM—NEGOTIATION: MASTERING THE ART OF THE
DEAL, by Morten Lund
ISBN: 978-1-888960-09-9, 149 pages,
US$15.95

Everyone negotiates. The question is not just
whether we negotiate, but whether we negotiate well. In his third book, Morten Lund, a Yale
Law graduate and experienced law partner,
offers 21 Rules for negotiation skill. With
Lund, go in prepared, and come out victorious.

For the Law Student

The Art Of The Law School Transfer: A Guide to Transferring Law Schools, By Andrew B. Carrabis and Seth D. Haimovitch
ISBN 978-1-888960-30-3, 160 pg, US$16.95

Transferring from one law school to another is like painting a panorama. There are the technical elements, sure. Failing to follow these can make colors sag and smear, destroying all that's done to that point. In law school, that's a lifetime of academic preparation. As with all works of art, there's an artistic element as well. It's not enough to simply submit papers and files on time. The transfer process is full of quirks that a novice—any novice—will not see coming. With this book new students will be prepared, and will prepare their own works of art. After years of effort and sacrifice, don't ruin a portrait with needless errors. Instead, create the masterpiece that will get you into the law school of your dreams.

Later-in-Life Lawyers: Tips for the Non-Traditional Law Student, by Charles Cooper
ISBN 978-1-888960-06-8, 288 pg, US$18.95

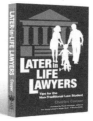

Law school is a scary place for any new student. For an older ("non-traditional") student, it can be intimidating as well as ill-designed for the needs of a student with children, mortgages, and the like. Includes advice on families and children; the LSAT, GPAs, application process, and law school rankings for non-traditional students; paying for law school; surviving first year; non-academic hurdles; and the occasional skeleton in the non-traditional closet. This book is a must-read for the law student who is not going directly from college to law school.

The Slacker's Guide to Law School: Success Without Stress, by Juan Doria
ISBN 978-1-888960-52-5, 162 pg, US$16.95

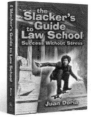

It is easy to fall into a trap of assuming that one either strives and succeeds or slacks and fails. Enjoying three years of law school is not the opposite of learning the law. There's also a tendency to follow a herd mentality: the assumption that there's just one right way to do something, or just one way to study the law. Too often, this involves too much make-work and too much stress. This book will show you how to do law school right: success without stress. (Or at least with *less* stress.)

LAW SCHOOL: GETTING IN, GETTING GOOD, GETTING THE GOLD,
by Thane Messinger
ISBN: 978-1-888960-80-8, 367 pages, US$16.95

The key in successful law study is a minimum
of wasted effort and a maximum of results. Still
outlining cases? A waste of time. Failing to use
hypotheticals? A dangerous omission.
Preparing a huge outline? A dangerous waste
of time. Don't waste your time, and don't
neglect what's truly important. Learn law school techniques that work.
Once you're in, Get Good, and Get the Gold!

THE INSIDER'S GUIDE TO GETTING A BIG FIRM JOB: WHAT EVERY LAW
STUDENT SHOULD KNOW ABOUT INTERVIEWING,
by Erika M Finn and Jessica T. Olmon
ISBN-13 978-1-888960-14-3, 130 pages,
US$16.95

The competition for top jobs is intense, and the
special needs of law firm recruiters are
unknown to most law students. Most books
aimed at law students speak to how to get into
law school, and how to succeed in law school, but none address how to
get a lucrative job. This book is an insider's look at the secrets of landing a dream law firm job.

PLANET LAW SCHOOL II: WHAT YOU NEED TO KNOW (BEFORE YOU GO)—
BUT DIDN'T KNOW TO ASK ... AND NO ONE ELSE WILL TELL YOU,
by Atticus Falcon
ISBN 978-1-888960-50-7, 858 pages, US$24.95

An encyclopedic reference. Examines hundreds
of sources, and offers in-depth advice on law
courses, materials, methods, study guides, professors, attitude, examsmanship, law review,
internships, research assistantships, clubs, clin-
ics, law jobs, dual degrees, advanced law
degrees, MBE, MPRE, bar review options, and the bar exam. Sets out all
that a law student must master to excel in law school.

For the Law Student

JAGGED ROCKS OF WISDOM: PROFESSIONAL ADVICE FOR THE NEW
ATTORNEY, by Morten Lund
ISBN: 978-1-888960-07-5, US$18.95

Written by a top partner, this no-nonsense
guide is a must-have for the new associate. Its
"21 Rules of Law Office Life" will help make
the difference to your success in the law: surviving your first years as an attorney, and
making partner. Beware. Avoid the dangers.
Read, read, and read again these 21 Rules of
Law Office Life.

JAGGED ROCKS OF WISDOM—THE MEMO: MASTERING THE LEGAL
MEMORANDUM, by Morten Lund
ISBN: 978-1-888960-08-6, US$18.95
This book focuses on one of the most complex
aspects of professional work for a new attorney: researching, drafting, and refining the
legal memorandum. This book breaks the
process of the legal memorandum into "21
Rules." In these rules the mysteries are
revealed. The process and survival will be no
less arduous, but with this book the journey
will not be as treacherous.

THE YOUNG LAWYER'S JUNGLE BOOK: A SURVIVAL GUIDE,
by Thane Messinger
ISBN 978-1-888960-19-1, US$18.95
A career guide for summer associates,
judicial clerks, and all new attorneys. Now in
its 14th year and second edition, hundreds of
sections with advice on law office life, advice
on law office life, including working with
senior attorneys, legal research and writing,
memos, contract drafting, mistakes, grammar,
email, managing workload, timesheets, annual

reviews, teamwork, department, attitude, perspective, working with
clients (and dissatisfied clients), working with office staff, using office
tools, and yes, much more.

Recommended in the ABA's *Law Practice Management* and *The
Compleat Lawyer,* as well as in numerous state bar journals.